Identifying and Growing Internal Leaders

A Framework for Effective Teacher Leadership

Kimberly T. Strike, Janis Fitzsimmons, and Rebecca Hornberger

ROWMAN & LITTLEFIELD
Lanham • Boulder • New York • London

Published by Rowman & Littlefield
An imprint of The Rowman & Littlefield Publishing Group, Inc.
4501 Forbes Boulevard, Suite 200, Lanham, Maryland 20706
www.rowman.com

6 Tinworth Street, London SE11 5AL, United Kingdom

British Library Cataloguing in Publication Information Available

Library of Congress Cataloging-in-Publication Data

Includes bibliographic references and index.
ISBN 978-1-4758-4657-7 (cloth : alk. paper)
ISBN 978-1-4758-4658-4 (pbk. : alk. paper)
ISBN 978-1-4758-4659-1 (Electronic)

∞™ The paper used in this publication meets the minimum requirements of American National Standard for Information Sciences—Permanence of Paper for Printed Library Materials, ANSI/NISO Z39.48-1992.

Printed in the United States of America

Contents

Foreword

There are no shortages of problems facing our schools and no individuals more critical to solving them than our teachers. Our frontline teachers face daily challenges of the impact of poverty, a growing population of students with special needs, a system hampered by lack of funding that in many instances forces them to supply their classrooms, increasing demands for accountability based on standardized test scores, and most recently, real concerns over their physical safety. While their commitment to their profession and compassion for their students is admirable, teachers cannot solve these problems in isolation. Tackling the toughest issues at the school level requires leadership, yet the traditional school leaders often find themselves mired in an overwhelming array of demands that render their efforts episodic and not systemic.

Principals' best intentions are frequently nullified by time necessary to deal with parent complaints, disciplinary matters, district meetings, and special-education staffings. While all of these are necessary, the principal finds that there is simply not enough time in the day for actually leading important initiatives to address the school's problems, to make progress on the goals, or to manage the change process. As a result, teachers make their best efforts with the students they have each year, and many persist. Others, however, choose to leave the profession to pursue a new career and we are finding that now there is a looming teacher shortage. Those who do stay in the profession and persist from year to year may be rewarded with movement on the salary schedule, but by and large do not have any career path that enables them to make an impact beyond their classrooms. If schools are to improve, if the big problems are to be solved, there must be structural changes that create conditions for new leaders to emerge and to lead. These new leaders cannot be more administrators; rather, they need to be teachers who are immersed in and thus best understand the challenges, needs, and priorities of the school.

As the saying goes, "If you always do what you've always done, you'll always get what you always got." Teacher leadership is a far cry from what we have always done, and *Identifying and Growing Internal Leaders: A Framework for Effective Teacher Leadership* will engage you in thinking deeply about what our schools, districts, communities, and beyond can get from creating conditions where teacher leaders can learn and grow, act, and lead. This book is an important work making a compelling case for teacher leadership and teacher leaders as a necessary role for tangible school improvement. This book is far more than a collection of success stories of teacher leaders making a difference. While it has the evidence and examples, the authors trace the origins of this key role and create a framework of teacher leader domains. From these four domains, teacher leadership competencies, relational leadership, instructional leadership, and management competencies, they outline a pathway from teacher to teacher leader. Additionally, the key characteristics for teacher leaders are posited and supported with evidence from the field. One can only conclude that when a school system embraces the concept of teacher leaders and creates the space for this new role, school-level growth, change, and improvement will flourish.

Glenn W. "Max" McGee

Preface

> Thanks to an abundance of research and documented practice, we know what to do. A heavy burden falls on the authors of this book to say that the 21st century really will be different. They must persuade you that their ideas provide an enduring framework that helps students find success and helps educators find meaning, purpose, and collegiality in a profession that has been beset by fragmentation and isolation. (Reeves 2007, 10)

Teacher leadership has a long history in education dating back to the turn of the century. Historically, teacher leadership has not been recognized in its own right, but thought of as an extension of teaching. In *Identifying and Growing Internal Leaders: A Framework for Effective Teacher Leadership*, the authors focus on the knowledge, skills, dispositions, and practices of effective teacher leaders. Through connections between theory and practice, and anchored in multiple sets of standards, competencies, and propositions, *The Framework* within the text was developed to assist in and support training for current and aspiring teacher leaders, teachers who work with teacher leaders, and district or building leaders who supervise or evaluate teacher leaders.

Some educational leaders don't have aspirations to become administrators. Some wish to remain in the classroom, but provide leadership at a different level: director, coordinator, department chair, lead teacher, dean, curriculum specialist, instructional coach, mentor, and such. Recognition of teacher leaders, accountability, and evaluation have resulted in:

- State endorsements or licensure reflecting specific training and licensing requirements; a need for school districts and school leaders to define

this tier of leadership and how this tier of leadership will be defined; recognition of roles held by teacher leaders; and determination of how they will be evaluated.
- A call for an evaluation resource in which teacher leaders can demonstrate proficiency, create goals to promote growth, and do so within a structure that reflects inter-rater reliability.
- A demand for data-driven decision-making strategies.
- Research that demonstrates how district and school leader effectiveness is directly related to increased student performance, school improvement, and reform initiatives.
- Importance for district and school leaders to have an understanding of the inter-relatedness of supervision, evaluation, and professional learning and growth.
- A need for educational leaders to understand that all district and school employees (including leaders, teacher leaders, teachers, and support staff) must have the opportunity to develop differentiated learning and growth plans. Resources must be allocated to support professional growth and development.
- A need for educational leaders to share a common language and knowledge of effective models for personal and professional growth, their relationship to national and state standards, and most importantly, to increase student performance.

Identifying and Growing Internal Leaders: A Framework for Effective Teacher Leadership offers both the framework and corresponding rubrics that reflect the Teacher Leader Model Standards (2011), The Teacher Leadership Competencies (2014), PSEL (2015), NELP (2018) standards, and NBPTS propositions (2016). Through practical and applied examination, teacher leaders are provided targets specific to them—their roles, their responsibilities, their competencies, and their standards. This is important for professional growth and development. It also provides common language and a common set of proficiencies specific to the evaluation of teacher leaders whether through self-evaluation or evaluation by a supervisor. To evaluate a teacher leader on a teacher evaluation or an administrator's evaluation does not capture the true identity, nor purpose, of teacher leaders; therefore, those evaluations specific to different roles or titles cannot be reliable or valid for a person serving as a teacher leader. An understanding of these differences is important, whether it is the administrator, board member, colleagues, or the teacher leader him/herself.

Identifying and Growing Internal Leaders: A Framework for Effective Teacher Leadership is helpful for aspiring administrators and teacher leaders, as well as teachers rooted in the classroom, to better understand how to maximize utilization of teacher leaders and procure ongoing professional learning at the district and school level. Both teacher leaders and administrators will find the elements within *The Framework* and alignment with standards helpful in self-reflection of personal and professional strengths, and areas in need of improvement. The four domains of *The Framework for Effective Teacher Leadership* are:

Domain 1—Critical Competencies
Domain 2—Professional Growth of Self and Others
Domain 3—Instructional Leadership
Domain 4—Advocacy

Each domain identifies components or building blocks reflective of knowledge, skills, dispositions, and practices of effective teacher leaders. These components are further relegated to elements that provide relevant conditions or requirements of the teacher leader. Rubrics for each element are provided for the user to discern placement on the continuum. As a continuum, movement may occur both forward and back as roles, responsibilities, and performance change. *The Framework* is anchored in standards (Teacher Leader Model Standards) and competencies, and links theory and experience (practice).

Identifying and Growing Internal Leaders: A Framework for Effective Teacher Leadership features illustrations (figures, tables, and text boxes), examples, discussion questions that stimulate application of concepts and enhance understanding of the chapter, the opportunity for self-assessment and reflection, and application into one's own placement. Chapters open with objectives that link teacher leadership competencies and skills to existing teacher leadership, leadership, and teaching standards, including Teacher Leader Model Standards (Teacher Leadership Exploratory Consortium 2008; National Education Association 2011), The Teacher Leader Competencies (Center for Teaching Quality, National Board for Professional Teaching Standards, and National Education Association 2014), Professional Standards for Educational Leaders or PSEL (2015), National Policy Board for Educational Administration or NELP (2018), National Board for Professional Teaching Standards five core propositions (2016), and other applicable state standards or recommendations. Summaries at the end of each chapter highlight critical points and especially salient issues specific to theory, practice, and application of teacher leadership.

Note that case studies are not part of this publication. To enhance the ability to and depth at which one could examine case studies, the authors felt it would be best to present them as a separate publication, and they can be found under separate cover as a companion text. The companion text allows the reader to view leveled case studies (elementary, middle school, secondary) as well as specialists, support personnel, and international examples.

REFERENCE

Ainsworth, L., et al. (2007). Ahead of the curve: The power of assessment to transform teaching and learning. D. Reeves (Ed.). Bloomington, IN: Solution Tree Press.

Acknowledgments

We are grateful to the teachers who serve as teacher leaders. We thank you for stepping up to serve our children, your colleagues, and your school. We thank you for being attuned to what needs to be done and just doing it, most often without recognition or additional monies. We thank you for being self-motivated to explore, learn, implement, fail, and succeed. And we thank you for inspiring those around you.

We are grateful to our colleagues who serve next to us and provide insight and confirmation, and further develop our understanding through questioning. We thank those who peer reviewed this publication. We are appreciative to those on whose shoulders we stand, building upon research and observations spanning over thirty years.

We are grateful to our families for their unconditional love, support, and patience while we act on our innovative spirits and contribute to our field. We love you!

Introduction

> Success is peace of mind which is a direct result of self-satisfaction in knowing you made the effort to become the best you are capable of becoming.
>
> —John Wooden, UCLA basketball coach from 1948–1975

While John Wooden is best known as a basketball coach, he was a teacher and a leader. His record of ten national championships featured four perfect seasons and eighty-eight straight wins. What most people don't realize is that he coached for twenty-eight years before he won a national championship, and the record that has made him a legend reflects only his last twelve years at UCLA. Wooden didn't focus on results, but instead on daily events that served as building blocks with the understanding that results would follow. Achieving excellence takes time, commitment, and laser-sharp focus on continuous improvement.

Teacher leadership is predicated upon engagement in the science of improvement. Teacher leaders are in a premier position in that they have the ability to see the system. This raw experience provides the opportunity to see gaps, needs, and interests of those categorized as stakeholders of our educational system: students, teachers, administration, and parents. Teacher leaders view data through its context, and provide intentional, focused responses to it with student and staff learning as the goal.

Improvement measures must be embedded in daily work. Data must be accessible in a timely manner, and those using the data must understand its purpose, uses, and reporting. Changes must be designed, implemented, and measured in a timely manner and for a specific purpose. Accountability must be determined prior to engagement in the improvement process, and boundaries clearly identified.

The improvement process must prove to be psychologically safe so those engaged in the process feel free to take risks and work outside the box without consequence, punitive punishment, or judgment, for it is often through failure that we propel forward. Teacher leaders are the change agents of our schools. They represent a gathering of the curious who do what needs to be done to impact student learning, their colleagues, and their schools.

Though teacher leaders have such impact, this group of professionals is often glazed over. They have expanded their skill sets, roles, and responsibilities beyond the framework for teaching but they are not recognized as administrators. Their roles are often absent of job descriptions or clarification of supervision, evaluation, or professional targets. Administrators often rely on them to share work, lead initiatives, or rally the forces but don't understand how to build capacity in one of the greatest resources available.

Therefore, *Identifying and Growing Internal Leaders: A Framework for Effective Teacher Leadership* provides the historic overview, research, and theoretical groundings foundational to understanding teacher leadership. More importantly, it provides professional targets anchored in teacher, leader, and teacher leader standards through the development of *The Framework* and the rubrics that align to it. These professional targets are embedded in the daily functions of teacher leaders. Through careful examination and selection, teacher leaders build capacity in themselves and others to foster improvement and effectively impact students, colleagues, and schools.

USING THIS BOOK

This book may be used in a variety of ways. For example, it may be used for a professional book talk, where as such, teacher leaders and those who work with, supervise, or evaluate them can use the book as a point of discussion. As a book talk it could be central to discussion focused on teacher leadership within your own district or school context. Questions could be developed to determine best use and alignment with the use of teacher leaders in a specific district or school.

It can be used to identify areas of need or interest when setting professional goals. Through self-reflection, teacher leaders can discern where they are at currently and where they need to be, and then set goals and identify resources to assist them with their specific journey.

As a mentoring or coaching tool, *The Framework* can be used by mentors or coaches to work with teacher leaders or teachers who aspire to become teacher leaders. Through examination of specific indicators and identification of level of performance for that indicator, one can set professional goals for improvement and growth.

As a PLC or team, *The Framework* can provide a springboard for professional learning by examining one component at each meeting, reflecting on current practices, sharing strategies and actions, implementing, and reporting back.

The chapters are written so they are self-contained and may be read out of order. Each chapter begins with objectives anchored in NELP, PSEL, MTLS standards and NBCPT propositions. Each chapter ends with a summary, self-assessment, and reflection, and references specific to that chapter.

The Framework for Effective Teacher Leadership

The Framework was developed over the course of three years. The authors were very intentional with the language chosen. The rubrics aligned to *The Framework* reflect four levels of performance with intentional language, specifically the verbs, chosen to foster growth and professional learning. As with Danielson's framework, there is an understanding that the teacher leader will visit but not remain within the top level of performance for all time, as *The Framework* reflects fluid levels of performance in accordance with changing roles and responsibilities.

The Framework for Effective Teacher Leadership has two main parts: *The Framework* and the rubrics that align with *The Framework*. The rubrics reflect each component within the four domains and are broken down to capture the essential information of the elements within that component. The rubric reflects the levels of performance for each of the elements. For the purpose of this book, the authors have coupled Domains 2 and 3 and Domains 1 and 4. Each will be reviewed in depth in future chapters.

After reviewing the literature and exploring standards associated with teacher leadership, the authors have structured the framework within four domains that reflect general areas of knowledge. There are fourteen components identified, each describing specific skills within the domain. Each component is broken down to explicit dispositions and practices of effective teacher leaders. There are fifty-six elements identified by the authors. Figures 4.1 and 4.2 provide *The Framework for Effective Teacher Leadership* in its entirety. This allows the reader to see the domains, components, and elements as a whole.

The domains are divided into quadrants. To examine the domains in order, the reader can begin at the top left, move to the top right, then lower right, and finally the bottom left to follow the domains in order of number. Within each domain are numbered components, and under the numbered components are bulleted elements. This allows the reader to move from the general knowledge category, to the subsets of skills in the components, to the elements that reflect the dispositions and practices required.

PURPOSE OF *THE FRAMEWORK FOR EFFECTIVE TEACHER LEADERSHIP*

The Framework for Effective Teacher Leadership was created for and by practitioners to guide preparation, hiring, learning, supervision and evaluation specific to teacher leaders. *The Framework* informs government policies and regulations that oversee the profession. By articulating the scope of work and the values that the profession stands for, standards suggest how practitioners can achieve the outcomes that the profession demands and the public expects. Professional standards are not static. They are regularly reviewed and adjusted to accurately reflect evolving understandings of, expectations for, and contexts that shape the profession's work.

The Framework is foundational to identify targets, provide commonality, explore opportunities, advocate for teacher leadership, evaluation, supervision, mentoring, coaching, and preparation of new leadership; it is a guide for professional learning for current leaders, as well as a roadmap for novice or aspiring teacher leaders, for identification of targets for school improvement, and for communication with the larger community.

CHAPTER OVERVIEW

In the paragraphs below, the focus of each chapter's content is summarized as a quick reference for the reader.

Chapter 1: A Comprehensive Examination of Teacher Leadership

To understand teacher leadership within the context of the district and school, this chapter provides an historic overview of teacher leadership. It explores multiple definitions of teacher leadership, as well as roles of those serving in this capacity. This chapter also looks at leadership in a comparative way to management, and relevant theories of both leadership and teacher leadership.

Chapter 2: Linking *The Framework for Effective Teacher Leadership* to Standards

Anchored in standards as developed, this chapter provides direct alignments between *The Framework* and three specific sets of standards: National Educational Leadership Preparation (NELP), Professional Standards for Educational Leaders (PSEL), and Teacher Leader Model Standards (TLMS).

Chapter 3: The Diversity of Teacher Leaders

This chapter explores the diverse roles and responsibilities of teacher leaders, as well as the selection process. Teacher leaders often hold positions or perform duties without formal appointment, assignment, or recognition; therefore, this chapter examines recognition of teacher leaders through the lens of administration and state agencies.

Chapter 4: Setting the Stage for *The Framework for Effective Teacher Leadership*

This chapter details the steps taken in the development of *The Framework* and provides the reader with a clear understanding of the format. The four domains, as well as an explanation of the levels of performance, are set forth. This chapter also establishes the necessity of *The Framework* as a tool for practitioners who are focused on continuous professional growth and improvement.

Chapter 5: *The Framework for Effective Teacher Leadership*: Domains 2 and 3

In order to assure a deep understanding of *The Framework*, this chapter provides a narrative description of Domain 2 (*professional growth of self and others*) and Domain 3 (*instructional leadership*). Furthermore, examples and clear definitions of skill levels are provided relating to the leadership practices set forth.

Chapter 6: *The Framework for Effective Teacher Leadership*: Domains 1 and 4

Mirroring the prior chapter, narrative explanations, as well as examples of specific practices and levels of skill, are explored for Domain 1 (*critical competencies*) and Domain 4 (*advocacy*) of *The Framework*.

Chapter 7: Professional Learning to Enhance Teacher Leadership

This chapter provides the reader with an in-depth look at the cyclical process of continuous improvement and professional growth for teacher leaders, explaining the key aspects of differentiated professional learning and self-renewal.

Chapter 8: The Research Behind *The Framework for Effective Teacher Leadership*

The final chapter of this text provides a clear overview of the research that has been conducted and that forms the basis for *The Framework for Effective Teacher Leadership*. Assumptions and attributes of *The Framework* are examined, as well as the study findings, limitations, data analysis, synthesis, and evaluation of the data.

RECOMMENDATIONS FOR THE FUTURE

The complexity of teacher leadership spotlights a unique group of people with a necessary set of skills. *The Framework for Effective Teacher Leadership* is a tool that provides job-embedded, professional targets specific to teacher leaders. Through reflection, participating in rich professional dialogue, and laser focus, teacher leaders are provided meaningful, measurable targets foundational to goal setting, growth, and learning.

REFERENCE

Danielson, C. (2007). *Enhancing professional practice: A framework for teaching* (2nd ed.). Alexandria, VA: ASCD.

Chapter One

A Comprehensive Examination of Teacher Leadership

OBJECTIVES

Throughout this chapter you will:

1. Explore a historic overview of teacher leadership (TLMS 4; NELP 4; PESL 4, 5, 6, and 7).
2. Examine varying definitions of teacher leadership (TLMS; NELP; PESL; NBPTS).
3. Investigate roles of teacher leadership (TLMS 6, 7; NELP 6; PESL 2; NBPTS 4, 5).
4. Differentiate leadership versus management (TLMS 6; NELP 6; PESL 5, 6, and 9).
5. Examine teacher leadership and leadership theories (TLMS 1; NELP 3; PESL 2 and 3).
6. Examine key qualities of effective teacher leadership (TLMS 4; NELP 2 and 3; PESL 2 and 3; NBPTS 1, 2, 3, 4, 5).
7. Identify the problem and significance to the field (TLMS 2; NELP 1; PESL 1 and 10; NBPTS 4).
8. Examine the conceptual framework (TLMS 7; NELP 1; PESL 1; NBPTS 4, 5).
9. Investigate questions and methodologies (TLMS 2, 4, 6; NELP 4 and 6; PESL 4, 6, and 7; NBPTS 4, 5).

HISTORIC OVERVIEW OF TEACHER LEADERSHIP

Consider Aristotle, Anne Sullivan, Maria Montessori, William McGuffy, Emma Willard, and Jaime Escalante. Each was a teacher—perhaps even a great teacher who had immeasurable impact on students. And each has a niche in the history of teaching and learning. But were they teacher leaders? The concept of the teacher leader dates back to the turn of the century, but it wasn't until the late 1980s and mid-1990s that the terminology gained notice in literature.

Miles, Saxl, and Lieberman (1988) examined teacher leaders to identify the qualities teacher leaders embodied as a result of taking on roles related to reform movements. Smylie (1995) reviewed more than two thousand articles on teacher leadership. Descriptions of the roles of teacher leaders were central to the articles he reviewed. Little (1995) explored the legitimacy of teacher leadership. Fullan (1995) wrote about the need to establish a culture for teacher leadership.

McLaughlin and Talbert (1993) talked about professional communities and teacher leadership. In each scenario, teacher leaders were found to be beneficial to educational enterprises. While literature focused on teacher leaders has a long history, the questions, concerns, and observations of thirty plus years ago could have very well been written today. There was then, and continues to be, a lack of an accepted and applied definition of the teacher leader.

The reality is that the teacher leader role is one that is often overlooked, misunderstood, and taken for granted. School administrators rely on teacher leaders to facilitate professional learning communities, chair curriculum committees, mentor new teachers and such, but administrators are often not formally trained nor encouraged to understand the capacity of teacher leaders. The roles and responsibilities of teacher leaders are dependent on the school's and district's level of recognition and utilization of teachers serving in such roles. However, the knowledge, skills, dispositions, and practices of effective teacher leadership are developed over time.

So, though an era has passed and initiatives such as A Nation at Risk, No Child Left Behind, Race to the Top, Common Core Standards, and teacher accountability have had an impact on teacher training and evaluation, the effective use of teacher leaders continues to be presented and questioned in the same way it has been in the past as more of an afterthought than a promising practice or policy. One challenge may be the lack of agreement on a definition of teacher leadership.

DEFINING TEACHER LEADERSHIP

Definitions of Teacher Leadership

The concept of teacher leadership lends itself to varying definitions that each validate the importance of, identify important skills within, and address roles of teacher leaders. The US Department of Education describes the concept of teacher leadership as "specific roles and responsibilities that recognize the talents of the most effective teachers and deploy them in service of student learning, adult learning and collaboration, and school and system improvement" (PEBC 2015).

Through a review of literature, one definitive finding emerged: the definition of teacher leadership remains to be agreed upon. It varies by study and researcher, as well as by state, local, national and international initiative. In an examination of definitions by study and researcher, we find the following examples:

- "Teachers are leaders when they function in professional communities to affect student learning; contribute to school improvement; inspire excellence in practice; and empower stakeholders to participate in educational improvement" (Childs-Bowen, Moller, and Scrivner 2000, p. 28). Furthermore, it is noted that enhancing teacher leadership can help schools and districts reach the following goals: "(1) Improve teacher quality; (2) Improve student learning; (3) Ensure that education reform efforts work; (4) Recruit, retain, motivate, and reward accomplished teachers; (5) Provide opportunities for professional growth; (6) Extend principal capacity; and (7) Create a more democratic school environment." (National Comprehensive Center for Teacher Quality 2007)
- York-Barr and Duke (2004, p. 288) defined teacher leadership as "the process by which teachers, individually or collectively, influence their colleagues, principals, and other members of school communities to improve teaching and learning practices with the aim of increased student learning and achievement."
- Danielson (2006, p. 12) refers to teacher leadership as "that set of skills demonstrated by teachers who continue to teach students but also have an influence that extends beyond their own classrooms to others within their own school and elsewhere. It entails mobilizing and energizing others with the goal of improving the school's performance of its critical responsibilities related to teaching and learning."
- Crowther, Fergeson, and Hann (2009, p. 10) state, "Teacher leadership is essentially an ethical stance that is based on views of both a better world

and the power of teachers to shape meaning systems. It manifests in new forms of understanding and practice that contribute to school success and to the quality of life of the community in the long run."

States define teacher leadership in many ways, too. Those definitions usually revolve around courses and competencies a teacher must meet to be credentialed as a teacher leader. Some states, such as Ohio, call for teachers to have a master's degree and a defined number of years in the classroom (four in Ohio) prior to obtaining an endorsement specific to teacher leadership. Coursework then highlights areas of the classroom and administration such as alignment of standards, curriculum, instruction, assessment, collaboration, instructional coaching, learning, teaching, educational leadership, or mentoring.

In Louisiana, teacher leader programs are performance based, and aspiring teacher leaders must meet all National Educational Leadership Preparation (NELP) and Louisiana state leadership standards. In addition, teachers must complete six graduate hours in school leadership. These two courses articulate into a full educational leadership program. The teacher leader program in Louisiana is aimed at teachers who do not want to become administrators, but still want to be leaders in their schools.

Similarly, Georgia adopted a policy in 2011 that created a state teacher-leader endorsement and Illinois redefined their teacher leader endorsement in 2012. In Georgia, teacher leader programs are performance based and must address seven leadership standards for teacher leaders as defined by GaPSC Teacher Leadership Program Standards (2011).

In Illinois, "teacher leader" is defined as an endorsement that sits on a professional teacher educator license and can only be earned after, or in combination with, completion of a master's degree. "The teacher leader endorsement will create a career path to retain and develop high-performing teachers for leadership roles; formalize, define, and build the competencies necessary for high-quality leadership to improve student learning; and recognize and encourage shared leadership and decision-making in schools to maximize outcomes for children"; the code identifies five standards around which preparation programs must prepare teacher leaders. (Illinois Administrative Code, 25.32).

In Iowa, teacher leader programs are also built around five standards that define teacher leaders, and in addition the development of such programs is tied to a compensation incentive for each district. A few roles they highlight for teacher leaders include:

- Encourage teachers to share their ideas and practices by building a relationship to decrease the teacher's resistance to engage in collaboration.
- Educate teachers about the advantages of collaboration and its simplicity.

- Clearly communicate the purpose and vision of school-wide collaboration and how it promotes teacher development. (Iowa Department of Education 2017)

Definitions vary, too, by district through both contractual agreement and informal arrangement. For example, Norwalk School District in Iowa was one of the first to apply for a state Teacher Leader and Compensation (TLC) grant, which the state plans to eventually give to all districts. Norwalk reports, "Since we first implemented TLC, we have changed job descriptions. We realized technology is huge so we now have a technology component. Some of the roles we had at the beginning we changed. It is ever adjusting. I don't know if it will ever be the same from year to year" (Iowa Department of Education, 2016).

In San Juan Unified School District, California, partners negotiated an article in the teacher's contract (Article 24—Creating and Sustaining a Collaborative Culture) with the teachers' union. "Shared responsibility and accountability for results are at the core of a continuous improvement model" (SJTA, p. 83). Furthermore, 24.04 of this article established leadership teams in all district schools made up of faculty and administration and further defined the characteristics, selection, roles, and compensation of the teams and leaders as well as such things as conflict resolution, site innovation, and collaborative decision making.

In School District 203, Naperville, Illinois, Career 203, also negotiated by contractual agreement, to carve out career pathways for teachers that create a lattice of opportunities. The lattice allows latitude for teachers to move up and across and take on roles that are sometimes formally labeled teacher leader and other times named by roles considered to be teacher leader roles. The contract also spells out compensation for additional work.

Recently, Georgia began encouraging professional learning communities composed of university and college partners, school districts, and state entities to "work collaboratively in recurring cycles of collective inquiry and action research to achieve better results for students" (Presentation by the Georgia Board of Standards to the Midwest edTPA Conference 2018). These collaborations of district, higher education, and state entities assert that continuous development of teachers leads to better student results and that professional development begins with individual professional-learning plans developed and launched with each candidate as they complete preparation. Teacher leader roles here are defined over time in these continuous development efforts.

Many teacher leader roles across the United States are now being revisited and redefined by states as they develop their ESSA plans and consider Title II funding (Chiefs for Change 2017).

At the national level, definitions for teacher leadership are born, too. An initiative known as Teach to Lead recognizes and promotes teacher leadership. Teach to Lead is an effort that began in 2014 through the US Department of Education as an initiative of the National Board for Professional Teaching Standards. The initiative has an expanding list of sponsors including Association for Supervision and Curriculum Development (ASCD). Teach to Lead focuses on providing a venue that creates both time and space for teachers to be innovators, to create solutions to problems, and to come to the table with ideas that will change the profession, change education, and change the world.

In a presentation about Teach to Lead, Ruthanne Buck stated:

> Fundamentally, teacher leadership is about teacher ideas. It's about empowerment. It's about creating mechanisms and space and a pulpit for teachers to drive the change in the profession. But a bigger part of this work is really about capitalizing on a movement . . . and understanding teacher leadership as a vehicle to make big changes, not just creating a structure for teacher leadership. Teacher leadership is not about the hybrid roles or changing policy, but about creating the space for teachers to develop ideas, asking them what they need, what they want, and how we create it. (Buck 2015)

With so many working definitions of teacher leadership, it is difficult to carefully research the impact of teacher leadership and it's no wonder that people don't fully understand the concept of maximizing use of internal teacher talent, much less moving districts to buy into this concept.

For the purpose of *The Framework for Effective Teacher Leadership* and research contributing to this study, "teacher leadership" is defined as: *Transformative action yielding significant and sustainable results through support by teachers to teachers to improve the effectiveness of teaching and learning, and promote and influence change to improve school and student outcomes.*

ROLES OF TEACHER LEADERS

While researchers have not reached consensus regarding a definition, there has been some agreement that teacher leadership can operate at both a formal and informal level in schools and that it includes leadership of an instructional, organizational, and professional development nature (York-Barr and Duke 2004). Within that broad spectrum, the roles of the teacher leader vary with state and local laws, policies, and procedures, as well as formal and informal agreements.

The US Department of Education states, "a Teacher Leader might share distributed leadership with the principal, direct a site-based research project, develop communities of practice, or design a peer evaluation and review system. . . . Teacher Leaders are crucial members of a school or district leadership team, and are personally and professionally responsible for a school's success. Teacher Leaders model the most important professional practices and habits of mind, including the school's core values" (US Department of Education, 2012, section IX-Appendix).

In *National Spotlight: Teacher Leadership Changing School* Systems, which featured *Progress: Teachers, Leaders and Students Transforming Education* by B. R. Williams, roles of teacher leaders were identified as: mentor/coach; leadership team member; department chair; curriculum specialist; instructional specialist; lead teacher; advocate for change; and policy leader (Williams 2015). While researchers have not reached consensus regarding a definition, there has been some agreement that teacher leadership can operate at both a formal and informal level in schools and that it includes leadership of an instructional, organizational, and professional-development nature (York-Barr and Duke 2004).

In a report to the Illinois Governor's Office (2016, 2), the P-20 Teacher and Leadership Effectiveness Committee identified specific roles as identified by teacher and principal surveys:

- Curriculum specialist (i.e., identifying, designing, and implementing curriculum and school/district improvement)
- Coach (instructional practice and methods)
- Mentor teacher (i.e., providing mentoring to new teachers or others in need of assistance)
- Department chair or lead teacher
- Content specialist (in a specific content area)
- Supervision of others, provided that a supervisory endorsement is not required for the position to which the teacher leader is assigned
- Program leaders (i.e., relative to the climate of the school and classroom, curriculum, instruction or assessment)
- Other areas of responsibility as identified by school districts.

These roles are similar to other studies, such as Lord and Miller (2000) and Teachers Network Leadership Institute (2006), who identified the following roles:

- Mentor or coach new teachers
- Develop and deliver professional-development activities

- Lead curriculum-standards committees
- Develop curriculum
- Lead school improvement initiatives
- Serve as department- or grade-level chairs
- Serve on school leadership teams
- Become a union chapter leader
- Serve on committees, task forces, etc.
- Respond to crises in the schools (e.g., serve as a substitute, student discipline, respond to teacher's instructional needs, etc.)
- Collect assessment data and help administrators and teachers use it for school improvement

Administrators have been hammered with initiatives, policies, and laws over the past two decades. What better support than an internal master teacher who has demonstrated expertise and knows the ins and outs of the district to address these roles? This is reflected in the roles reported as Managerial and Master Teacher levels in Waves One, Two, and Three identified by Holland, Eckert, and Allen (2014) as shown in figure 1.1.

In response to each federal initiative, teachers have been tapped to play additional roles that address new school and district needs brought on by the federal initiatives. However, the system often fails to demonstrate the growth and actual usage of teacher leaders and their impact on policy and practice. Holland, Eckert, and Allen (2014) added this dimension, referring to teacher leader practices as the Fourth Wave.

The spectrum of roles delineated in this model demonstrate the need for school administrators to work with teacher leaders to develop their leadership

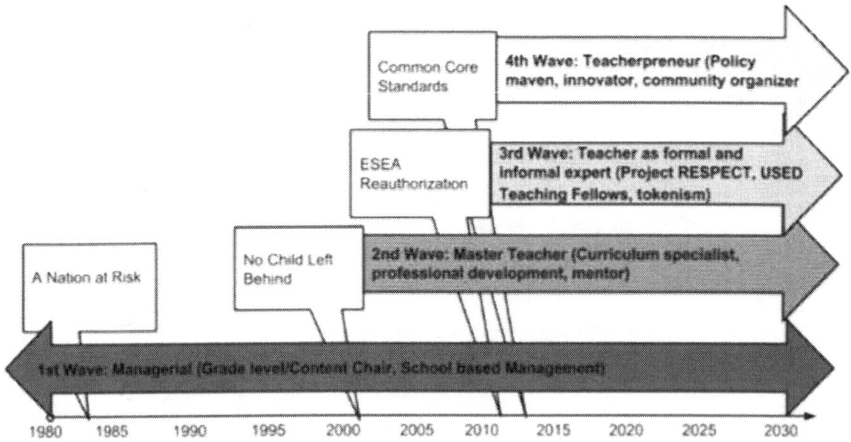

Figure 1.1. Federal Education Reform and Waves of Teacher Leadership
Holland, Eckert, and Allen (2014).

potential, as well as their managerial and master teacher expertise, and use teacher leaders in areas such as policy (local, state, and national), innovation, and organization movement to advance educational organizations as successful businesses do.

As the roles of teacher leaders are implemented, critical questions must be answered, too. Here are just a few:

- How much time should teacher leaders spend in and out of the classroom?
- How can leadership needs of the school/district be balanced with assigned teacher duties?
- What are the duties assigned, and what might other duties as assigned include?
- How should teacher leaders be evaluated? As a teacher, or administrator? Tied to performance in what ways? Who sets the goals? What evidence is needed? And by whom should this evaluation be completed?
- Is there a financial stipend, salary increment, load or contract with the additional or altered duties delineated?
- To what degree and in what realms do teachers have a voice in development of policy?

LEADERSHIP VS. MANAGEMENT

In all leader roles, there is both a management and a leadership component. For teacher leaders, many of the responsibilities are delegated, inherited, or assigned to teacher leaders and are management in nature. When one looks at the management behaviors, we see such tasks as:

- Planning
- Budgeting
- Organizing
- Staffing
- Problem solving
- Measuring
- Controlling (Kotter 2012, 28)

These behaviors are evident in the roles and responsibilities of teacher leaders, help events and activities to run smoothly, and prove to be managerial in nature. Running Professional Learning Communities, serving as a lead teacher, joint lesson planning, or analyzing data all require attention to managerial tasks relevant to and commonly performed by teacher leaders.

However, just as in any leader role, we must look to balance managerial behaviors with leadership behaviors. When we look at leadership behaviors, they go beyond organizing an event or running a meeting. Leadership calls for us to vision and produce change:

- Establish direction
- Align people
- Motivate and inspire
- Mobilize people to achieve astonishing results
- Propel us into the future (Kotter 2012, 29)

It is imperative we both understand the difference between these behaviors, and weigh the tendency to overmanage teacher leaders in order to create opportunities for teacher leaders to engage in true leadership that is essential to creating effective and great leaders and the improvement and advancement of the organization—ultimately, in schools that means student learning.

TEACHER LEADERSHIP AND LEADERSHIP THEORIES

A number of terms have been used to identify educational leadership theories. Leithwood, Jantzi, and Steinbach (1999) and Bush (2009) grouped leadership into models and identified them as: managerial, participative, transformational, interpersonal, transactional, postmodern, contingency, moral, and instructional. The model names are descriptive of the theories. Most recently, *instructional leadership* has become the foremost exemplar of a leader. It implies very explicitly that the focus of leadership is on teaching and learning and that teaching and learning are central to the work of the effective educational leader.

In contrast, other theories focus on characteristics of the leader such as moral leadership on values, beliefs, and ethics, or on "how" decisions are made as with participatory and democratic theories. *Distributed leadership* is a theory of educational leadership that is held in highest regard today even though its roots go back some eighty years. Distributed leadership combines aspects of participative and democratic leadership along with collaborative and shared leadership. Distributed leadership also aligns with Kotter's (2012) idea of creating a "leadership-centered culture" in an organization.

"Institutionalizing a leadership-centered culture is the ultimate act of leadership" (Kotter, 1999, p. 65). Applied to business, this means that companies value "decentralized leadership" and create additional leadership positions that provide opportunities for young people in their organizations to align with the company's vision and advance the work of the company and grow leadership to develop professionally at the same time. Companies like "Johnson and Johnson, Hewlett Packard, 3M and General Electric" (Kotter 1999, p. 64) have all benefited from this leadership theory.

For schools and districts, that means encouraging teacher leadership and valuing shared decision making provide the opportunity to engage a multiplicity of talented teachers with critical school and district initiatives that together advance the understanding and effectiveness of teaching and learning in schools while simultaneously developing professionally. In both scenarios, business and education organizations enhance the opportunity for growth, development, and success of their units by decentralizing leadership to increase the number of opportunities for people to take on leadership and grow personally and professionally and advance the organization.

KEY QUALITIES OF EFFECTIVE TEACHER LEADERSHIP

Qualities of teacher leaders are defined in part by standards such as the NELP and Professional Standards for Educational Leadership (PSEL) and NCPDI-ELCC Educational Leader Standards. Chapter 2 will discuss these in depth.

In 2008, the Teacher Leader Exploratory Consortium set out to identify teacher leader model standards that were defined as "the knowledge, skills and competencies that teachers need to assume leadership roles in their schools, district and the profession" (2008, p. 13). In 2010, the consortium released its draft standards for public comment. Seven domains frame the standards and describe the various qualities or dimensions of teacher leadership. The domains include:

- *Domain I: Fostering a collaborative culture to support educator development and student learning*
- *Domain II: Accessing and using research to improve practice and student learning*
- *Domain III: Promoting professional learning for continuous improvement*
- *Domain IV: Facilitating improvements in instruction and student learning*
- *Domain V: Promoting the use of assessments and data for school and district improvement*
- *Domain VI: Improving outreach and collaboration with families and community*
- *Domain VII: Advocating for student learning and the profession* (2010, p. 9)

Each domain is then deconstructed to identify what the consortium terms as functions—a delineation of the characteristics within a specific cluster or group of teacher leader qualities. For example, in domain I, the first function is, "Uses group processes to help colleagues work collaboratively to solve problems, make decisions, manage conflict and promote meaningful change" (2010, p. 14).

THE PROBLEM AND SIGNIFICANCE

While TLMS and competencies are identified, a comprehensive resource outlining a framework, clear expectations, identification of levels of performance (rubrics), and the provision of specific expectations at varying levels is not currently available. In an effort to gain understanding specific to criteria, selection, roles, responsibilities, preparation, and training of current teacher leaders, we conducted research as described below. This text was borne out of that study and documents the development of a comprehensive resource that provides the opportunity for teacher leaders to set goals and engage in professional conversation with administrators and supervisors to experience the type of professional growth that in turn improves teaching and learning.

Teacher leaders' responsibilities do not readily fit or align with most rubrics for current teacher evaluations, nor are they provided with specific expectations from which they can develop professional leadership goals. This leads to the question, "How is one to grow his/her professional skill sets if there is a moving target, or worse yet, no target at all?"

If the power of teacher leadership is to fuel school success, it is imperative to create and share an evaluation plan and instrument that frames the roles and responsibilities of teacher leaders and encourages growth and development in these leadership roles. This tool must recognize the difference between being a teacher, an administrator, or other leadership label, and focus on the teacher leader as a bridge between classroom teachers and building administrators. Teacher leaders must be recognized as the group of educators they are—those who have made the conscious decision to lead from the classroom.

The development of *The Framework for Effective Teacher Leadership* is focused on professional growth and development of teacher leaders. The tool and its associated resources serve to inform educational leaders and board members of the need for, uses of, and benefits of utilizing teacher leaders. In addition, the tool serves as a resource to advocate for teacher leaders who are now recognized within a separate endorsement area in some states.

CONCEPTUAL FRAMEWORK

A visual interpretation of the conceptual framework for teacher leadership is available in figure 1.2. In teacher leadership, driving initiatives are directly connected to the mission, vision, and goals of the district (or school, depending on the structure). Also in this foundational piece is the planning. Core values are separate but embedded in the foundation, as these drive our interactions and actions.

The pillars that uphold and support the work of the teacher leader are analysis, action, intensive support, and accountability. The area of *analysis*

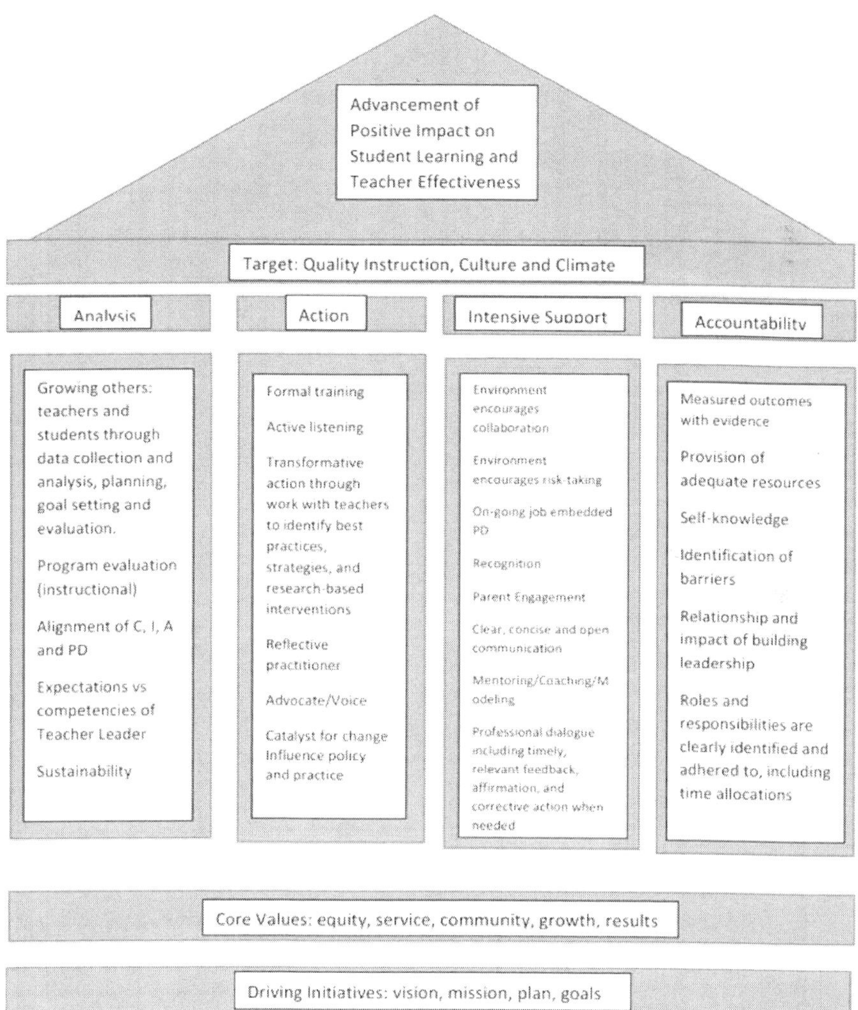

Figure 1.2. Conceptual Framework of Teacher Leadership

Strike, K. (2017). Adapted from "The Teacher Leader Competency Framework," by Leading Educators (2015), Washington, DC.

focuses on growing others through data collection and analysis, planning, goal setting, and evaluation. This analysis is required whether working with adults (teachers) or students. This area also focuses on program evaluation (instructional); alignment of curriculum, instruction, assessment, and professional development; expectations versus competencies of teacher leader; and sustainability. Therefore, this section requires the teacher leader to be critical, diagnostic, methodical, and rational.

The next pillar, *action*, calls for transformative practices, whether it be training, listening, coaching, modeling, improving one's own practice as a reflective practitioner, or involvement in executing or changing policy at various levels. The *intensive support* reflects engagement and encouragement supplied by teacher leaders. This area addresses collaboration, risk-taking, coaching, mentoring, engagement with parents and other community members, job-embedded professional development, and recognition of accomplishments.

The last pillar focuses on *accountability*. Starting with self and moving through a continuum that includes outcomes, resources, roles, responsibilities, impact of building leadership and barriers, this pillar requires the teacher leader to recognize and hold accountable the entities involved to move toward the target of quality instruction, culture, and climate. The ultimate goal is teacher leader impact on the positive advancement of students, colleagues and district/school. Evidence includes an increase in student learning, teacher effectiveness, or change of district policy.

QUESTIONS AND METHODOLOGIES

There were three methodologies used: focus groups, survey, and interviews. The focus groups were held as extensions of Teach to Lead summits during the 2016–2017 school year. Teach to Lead started in 2014 as a concerted effort of the US Department of Education, Association for Supervision and Curriculum Development, and National Board for Professional Teaching Standards with a specific focus on teacher leadership. These were national summits that took place in different locations throughout the United States.

Although the participation rate was low (N=21), it did represent a cross-section of participants from across the nation representing twelve states[1] and the District of Columbia. The focus groups reflected convenience sampling as all members of the focus groups were participants of the larger summit but carved time out of their busy schedules to provide voice, feedback and insight. Participants included teachers, teacher leaders, building- and district-level administrators, and state-level and higher-education representatives.

It was through focus groups that the initial framework was developed. The initial framework categorized all standards, competencies, and propositions, creating quite a lengthy document with very small font. It would be impossible for anyone to prove effective in all areas of the initial document even over a forty-year career. Through the voices of the teachers, teacher leaders, administrators, state-level educators, and other positions represented, the participants coded the initial document with stars, exclamation points, strikeouts, marginal notes, questions, and comments. This data were then analyzed and clustered to pare the initial document down to what is reflected in the current framework.

A second methodology used was survey (N=40). A survey of twenty-one questions electronically collected data throughout a one-year period (October 2016–October 2017) with sixteen respondents through social media and twenty-four through a web link. The survey reflected convenience sampling with a different set of participants than those participating in the focus groups, and represented nine states[2] and New Zealand. The survey collected data specific to the criteria, selection, roles, responsibilities, preparation, and training of teacher leaders in the participants' district/school as well as perceptions of national, state, and local support of teacher leadership.

A third methodology used was interviews. There were eight interviews conducted in Fall 2017 specific to the impact of teacher leaders on students, colleagues, and the district/school. Through purposive sampling, interviews were focused on those serving as, or with direct knowledge of, teacher leaders who had an impact on one or more of these identified areas. Participants included some contributors from the Teach to Lead summits, some enrolled in formal teacher-leader programs earning endorsement, and others were obtained through word of mouth and networking. Two states, Illinois and Ohio, are represented in the interviews.

The interview protocol was designed to delve deeper into specific areas explored in the survey and focus groups, but with different participants. This allowed participants' rich descriptions of experience (Denzin, 1989). To achieve this, open-ended questions were constructed to allow participants the freedom to share what was important to them, and at a depth that captured their connection to the question.

Furthermore, it allowed for passion and/or interest specific to that particular question in a way that reflects each participant's own understanding of the question as well as his or her knowledge and experience of that particular area. The content of questions focused participants' attention on the same areas addressed to different groups through other methods (survey and focus groups). The researcher utilized predesigned questions with multiple parts, and probed or provided follow-up questions for clarity or elaboration to initial replies.

It was through the use of the focus groups, survey, and interviews in the aforementioned that *The Framework for Effective Teacher Leadership* was born. *The Framework* is focused on scaffolding skills that both allow teacher leaders to function as effective leaders and identify opportunities for teachers to grow and develop as teacher leaders.

The tool and its associated resources serve to inform educational leaders and board members of the need for, uses of, and benefits of utilizing teacher leaders. In addition, the tool serves as a resource to advocate for teacher leaders who are now recognized within a separate endorsement area in some states.

SUMMARY

History shows the path of teacher leadership has been rough and challenging, yet teacher leadership holds promise to affect both school and student success. Prior to reform taking place, there must be a shared understanding of teacher leadership. While we realize that local schools and districts bring their own nuance to the concept, *The Framework* asserts that the definition of teacher leadership we have advanced is necessary to maximizing the potential of teacher leaders to positively impact student learning, colleagues, and schools/districts. This understanding does not necessarily mean uniformity across districts as districts will continue to utilize teacher leaders specific to the needs within their own communities.

Second, we highlight opportunities for teachers, parents, boards, and administrators to see how teacher leadership can impact students and schools. This includes assistance with acquisition of new skills, advancement of one's career, participation in decision making, development of climate that encourages continuous learning and improvement, promotion of voice, identification of channels of leadership to those who don't wish to become principals or superintendents, participation in research, and advocating through policy, procedure, and practice.

Third, we advance the importance of an instrument that frames developing skill sets along a continuum beyond the traditional teacher classroom role to leadership that nurtures the teacher, the educational organization, and its mission—student learning.

SELF-ASSESSMENT AND REFLECTION

1. The Cambridge Dictionary says that "definition" is a description of the features and limits of something. In other words, what it is and what it is not. Write your own definition of teacher leadership.

2. Consider Aristotle, Anne Sullivan, Maria Montessori, William McGuffy, Emma Willard, and Jaime Escalante. Were they teacher leaders? (You may have to look these educators up and find out a little more about them.) Explain your rationale.
3. What roles do you see in your school or district? To which teacher leader roles so you aspire?
4. Access the questions from the survey and interview (Appendices A and B) and see how your responses align with the participants in the study described here as you read on.

NOTES

1. States represented in the focus groups include FL, MO, OR, OK NY, VA, IL, CA, AL, KY, WA, WI, and the District of Columbia.
2. States represented through completion of the survey include NY, CA, NC, IL, OH, MD, NE, MN, and PA.

REFERENCES

Buck, R. (2015, July 16). This is #TeachtoLead. Retrieved from https://www.youtube.com/watch?v=o4rlENK-k5I&feature=youtu.be on

Bush, T. (2009, November). Leadership development and school improvement: Contemporary issues in leadership development. *Educational Review, 61*(4), 375–389.

Chiefs for Change. (2017, June 6). The case for teacher leaders. Retrieved from http://chiefsforchange.org/policy-paper/4658/

Childs-Bowen, D., Moller, G., and Scrivner, J. (2000, May). Principals: Leaders of Leaders. *NASSP Bulletin, 84*(616), 27–34.

Crowther, F., Fergeson, M., and Hann, L. (2009). *Developing teacher leaders* (2nd ed.). Thousand Oaks, CA: Corwin Press.

Danielson, C. (2006). *Teacher leadership that strengthens professional practice*. Alexandria, VA: Association of Supervision and Curriculum Development (ASCD).

Denzin, N. K. (1989). *Interpretive interactionism*. Newbury Park, CA: Sage Publications.

Fullan, M., and Hargreaves, A. (1996). *What's worth fighting for?* New York: Teachers College Press.

GaPSC Teacher Leadership Program Standards. (2011). Retrieved from https://www.gapsc.com/Commission/policies_guidelines/Downloads/Teacher_Leadership_Standards.pdf

Holland, H., Eckert, J. and Allen, M. (2014, December 24). From pre-service to teacher leadership: Meeting the future in educator preparation. P 433-445. Retrieved from http://www.tandfonline.com/doi/abs/10.1080/01626620.2014.977738

Hurst, B. (2016, March). So, you want to be a teacher leader? Retrieved from http://www.teachingquality.org/content/so-you-want-be-teacher-leader

Iowa Department of Education. (2016, April 11). Developing a TLC program that (really) works. Retrieved from https://www.educateiowa.gov/article/2016/05/17/developing-tlc-program-really-works

———. (2017, December 5). Key to successful teacher leadership is collaboration. Retrieved from https://www.educateiowa.gov/article/2017/12/05/key-successful-teacher-leadership-collaboration

Kotter, J. P. (2012). *Leading change*. Boston, MA: Harvard Business Review.

———. (1999). *John P. Kotter on what leaders really do?* Boston, MA: Harvard Business Press.

Leithwood, K., Jantzi, D., and Steinbach, R. (1999). *Changing leadership for changing times*. Buckingham: Open University Press.

Lieberman, A., Saxl, E., and Miles, M. (1988). Teacher leadership, ideology and practice. In Ann Lieberman (Ed.), *Building a Professional Culture in Schools* (pp. 300–877). New York: Teachers College Press.

Little, J. W. (1995). Contested ground: The basis of teacher leadership in two restructuring high schools. *The Elementary School Journal, 96*(1), 47–63.

Louisiana State Department of Education. (2011). Teacher leader endorsement. Retrieved from https://www.teachlouisiana.net/pdf/teacherleader_proposal.pdf

Lord, B., and Miller, B. (2000). *Teacher leadership: An appealing and inescapable force in school reform?* (Commissioned paper for the Department of Education, National Commission on Math and Science Teaching for the 21st Century). Newton, MA: Education Development Center.

Merz, S. (2014, June). Teacher leader versus "teacher" leader and why it matters. Retrieved from http://www.teachingquality.org/content/blogs/sandy-merz/teacher-leader-versus-teacher-leader-and-why-it-matters

McLaughlin, M. W., and Talbert, J. E. (1993). *Contexts that matter for teaching and learning: Strategic opportunities for meeting the nation's education goals*. Stanford, CA: Center for Research on the Context of Secondary School Teaching.

Millwater, J. and Ehrich, L. (2009). *Teacher leadership: Interns crossing to the domain of higher professional learning with mentors?* Australian Teacher Education Association, Paper presented at the Annual Conference of the Australian Teacher Education Association (ATEA) (Albury, June 28–July 1, 2009).

National Comprehensive Center for Teacher Quality. (2007, September 30). Key issue: Enhancing teacher leadership. Retrieved from https://eric.ed.gov/?id=ED543545

Public Education and Business Coalition. (2015). *Why teacher leadership?* Denver, CO: PEBC.

Rachel, C. (February 2013). *Finding a new way: Leveraging teacher leadership to meet unprecedented demands*. Washington, DC: Aspen Institute.

Reeves, D. (2007). *Ahead of the curve: The power of assessment to transform teaching and learning*. Bloomington, IN: Solution Tree Press.

Sheppard, B., Hurley, N., and Dibbon, D. (2010). Distributed leadership, teacher morale, and teacher enthusiasm: Unravelling the leadership pathways to school success. Memorial University of Newfoundland. Paper presented at the American Educational Research Association, Denver, Colorado, May 2010.

Sinha, S., Hanuscin, D., Rebello, C., Muslu, N., and Cheng, Y. (2012). *Confronting myths about teacher leadership*. V3:2. Columbia: University of Missouri.

Smylie, M. A., Lazarus, V., and Brownlee-Conyers, J. (1996, Fall). Instructional outcomes of school-based participative decision making. *Educational Evaluation and Policy Analysis, 18*(3), 181–198.

Soglin, A. and Hunt, E. (2016). *Teacher leadership report*: P-20 Teacher and leadership effectiveness committee. Springfield, IL: Illinois P-20 Council.

San Juan Teachers Association Contract. (2004). Article 24: Creating and sustaining a collaborative culture (pp. 90–92). Retrieved from http://www.sjta.org/docs/Contract_pdf/Article_24.pdf

State of Georgia. (2011). GaPSC teacher leadership program standards. Retrieved from https://www.gapsc.com/Commission/policies_guidelines/Downloads/Teacher_Leadership_Standards.pdf

State of Louisiana Standards for Teacher Certification. (2018). Louisiana standards for state certification of school personnel. Retrieved from http://www.doa.louisiana.gov/osr/lac/28v131/28v131.doc

Strike, K., Fitzsimmons, J. and Hornberger, R. (2018). *Identifying and growing internal leaders: A framework for effective teacher leadership*. Lanham, MD: The Rowman and Littlefield Publishing Group, Inc.

Teacher Leadership Exploratory Consortium. (2008, 2011). Teacher leader model standards. Washington, DC: National Education Association (NEA).

US Department of Education. (2012, February). Section IX-Appendix: Sample teacher role structure. Retrieved August 15, 2018, from https://www.ed.gov/teaching/national-conversation/vision/section-ix-appendix-sample-teacher-role-structure

US Department of Education. (2012). *The RESPECT project: Envisioning a teaching profession for the 21st century*. Washington, DC: US Department of Education.

Williams, B. R. (2015, August 6). Progress: Teachers, leaders and students transforming education. National spotlight: Teacher leadership changing school systems. Washington, DC: US Department of Education. Retrieved from http://sites.ed.gov/progress/2015/08/national-spotlight-teacher-leadership-changing-school-systems/

York-Barr, J., and Duke, K. (2004, Fall). What do we know about teacher leadership? Findings from two decades of scholarship. *Review of Educational Research, 74*(3), 255–316.

Chapter Two

Linking *The Framework for Effective Teacher Leadership* to Standards

OBJECTIVES

Throughout this chapter you will:

1. Explore National Educational Leadership Preparation (NELP) standards and connections to *The Framework* (NELP 1, 2, 3, 4, 5, 6, 7).
2. Explore Professional Standards for Educational Leadership (PSEL) standards and connections to *The Framework* (PSEL 1, 2, 3, 4, 5, 6, 7, 8, 9, 10).
3. Explore Teacher Leader Model Standards (TLMS) and connections to *The Framework* (TLMS 1, 2, 3, 4, 5, 6, 7).

NELP STANDARDS AND CONNECTIONS TO *THE FRAMEWORK*

The National Policy Board for Educational Administration (NPBEA) is an organization that was put into place in order to work toward a common understanding and articulation of what high-quality educational-leadership-preparation programs look like and how they should be structured. The NPBEA was created in response to a series of recommendations that were set forth from the 1987 report of the National Commission on Excellence in Educational Administration (National Policy Board for Educational Administration n.d.).

The report provided by this commission specified that the NPBEA would serve the following functions:

> Monitor the implementation of the Commission's recommendations; conduct periodic national reviews of preparation for educational administrators and

> professors; encourage the development of high quality programs for preparation of educational administrators; produce white papers on critical national policy issues in education; hold forums for discussions of issues in educational administration; and generally ensure good communication across interest groups about policy concerns. (University Council for Educational Administration 1987, 28)

The work of this commission and NPBEA are critical pieces in assuring that preparation programs are meeting leadership needs in the field and that candidates exit these programs fully prepared to take up the mantle of leadership.

The National Educational Leadership Preparation (NELP) standards were approved by NPBEA in 2017, and they are used to "guide the design, accreditation review, and state approval of preparation programs for principals and superintendents" (National Policy Board for Educational Administration n.d.). The NELP standards align to the Professional Standards for Educational Leaders (PSEL Standards), which are national standards outlining the essential knowledge and skills of educational leaders.

Essentially, the NELP standards provide guidelines for preparation programs, while the PSEL standards set forth the essential qualities of a practicing educational leader. While most often applied to the roles of the building principal and superintendent, both the NELP and PSEL standards include elements that also speak to the role of the teacher leader. That overlap becomes even more evident as we examine a crosswalk between both the building-level and district-level NELP standards.

The NELP standards for district-level leaders set forth the specific required knowledge base for entry-level district leaders, while the NELP standards for building-level leaders reflect the essential competencies for entry-level building leaders. Both sets of standards are divided into eight areas that are identified as standards. In the sections that follow, NELP standards will be discussed as they relate to both district-level and building-level leadership. Furthermore, these standards will be examined in relation to domains, components, and elements within *The Framework for Effective Teacher Leadership* in order to identify the areas of alignment when comparing the NELP standards and elements to *The Framework.*

NELP Standard 1 and Connections to *The Framework*

NELP standard 1 for both building-level and district-level leaders speaks to mission, vision, and core values of leaders. Specifically, the mission and vision should advance the success and well-being of all school stakeholders including students, building-level employees, and district-level employees (NELP element 1.1 for district-level and building-level leaders). In addition, the leader should inculcate the core values into all aspects of the district and building culture.

These values must hold student success, equity, social justice, caring, openness, inclusiveness, and trust at the core of this culture, and the school and district must create, evaluate, and sustain systems that are based on these essential core values (NELP element 1.2 for district-level and building-level leaders and NELP element 1.3 for building-level leaders). Furthermore, NELP element 1.3 for district-level leaders and element 1.4 for building-level leaders encompasses all aspects of improvement at both the school and district levels. This continuous improvement must be (a) the result of careful analysis, (b) based upon data that reveals the needs of all stakeholders, and (c) sustainable throughout time.

NELP standard 1 is in alignment with many areas of *The Framework for Effective Teacher Leadership*. For example, domain 1, *critical competencies*, includes component 1a, which speaks to the need for teacher leaders to advance the mission, vision, and goals of the school, and component 1d discusses effective coaching skills that ensure trust, confidentiality, respect, and appropriate and effective communication. Furthermore, 2b and 2c call out the importance of initiating and encouraging growth of self and others while also engaging and supporting the growth of future leaders.

In addition, domain 3 of *The Framework for Effective Teacher Leadership* addresses areas of instructional leadership that are also noted as key aspects of NELP standard 1. These areas include demonstrating effective use of assessments, implementing and supporting data-informed practices, providing an effective instructional program, and demonstrating purposeful planning that assures that every student is able to meet rigorous learning goals.

Finally, component 4c of *The Framework for Effective Teacher Leadership* calls on teacher leaders to support local change initiatives that address accountability, responsibility, fidelity of evaluation, and ensure learner growth and advancement of the profession.

NELP Standard 2 and Connections to *The Framework*

NELP standard 2 for both district-level and building-level leaders sets forth the essential aspects of ethics and professionalism for leaders at the beginning of their careers. Element 2.1 within both sets of standards speaks to the professional norms that are essential aspects of leadership roles. Specifically, integrity, fairness, transparency, and trust must be placed at the forefront of all actions, decision making, and relationships with stakeholders.

Element 2.2 for district-level leaders and element 2.4 for building-level leaders calls on leaders to model the ethical behavior expected of all school employees, while element 2.3 for district-level leaders sets forth the expectation that any unethical and unprofessional behavior is addressed in an appropriate manner throughout the whole of the organization. Finally, element 2.4 for district leaders and element 2.3 for building leaders speaks to the essential leadership practice of modeling and upholding the essential educational values of "democracy, community, individual freedom and responsibility, equity, social justice, and diversity" (NELP Standards for District-Level Leaders and Building-Level Leaders 2017).

We also find numerous areas of alignment within NELP standard 2 when comparing it with *The Framework for Effective Teacher Leadership*. First, component 1d, models effective coaching skills, maintains that effective teacher leaders establish an environment of trust, confidentiality, and respect with colleagues and staff members. In addition, component 2b within *The Framework* speaks to the importance of continuous improvement, as does element 2.1 within the NELP standards.

Component 4c within *The Framework* also addresses creating and supporting change, modeling accountability and responsibility, the importance of collaborative practices, and the importance of adhering to effective evaluation processes with fidelity.

NELP Standard 3 and Connections to *The Framework*

NELP standard 3 for both district-level and building-level leaders speaks to the essential elements of equity and cultural leadership both at the building level and throughout the district as a whole. Element 3.1 of both standards explains the equitable protocols, policies, practices, and systems that should be in place throughout the educational environment to ensure that all stakeholders are treated with fairness, respect, and with an understanding of culture and context.

Equitable access to resources, support, effective instruction and teachers, and learning opportunities is the focus of element 3.2 of the NELP standards for both district-level and building-level leaders. In addition, element 3.3 for both sets of standards delineates the types of culturally responsive practices that must be put into place by both district-level and building-level leaders.

Specifically, these practices include recognizing, confronting, and changing "institutional biases of student marginalization, deficit-based schooling, and low expectations associated with race, class, culture and language, gender and sexual orientation, and disability or special status" (NELP Standards for District-Level Leaders and Building-Level Leaders 2017).

Finally, element 3.4 of the NELP standards speaks to the district culture that must be cultivated by successful district-level leaders in order to meet the full range of student learner needs. Element 3.4 for building-level leaders calls for a supportive school community that assures all students and their families are treated with fairness and respect that is free from bias.

The Framework for Effective Teacher Leadership correlates with NELP standard 3 in multiple areas. This correlation is particularly strong with domain 3 of *The Framework*, which addresses instructional leadership. In particular, component 3a points out the importance of the effective use of assessments and compliance with local, state, and federal reporting requirements in order to assure growth and achievement for all students.

Component 3c of *The* Framework specifies the critical aspects of providing an effective instructional program, which includes the importance of providing teachers with time and training to appropriately administer assessments, as well as adapting instruction and advocating for instruction that supports all learners. Component 3d of *The Framework* speaks to purposeful planning that engages teacher leaders in assuring that the needs of diverse learners are met in all aspects of the classroom environment.

Finally, component 4b sets forth the expectation that teacher leaders demonstrate an understanding of educational policy, including understanding and responding to the larger context, evaluating the moral and legal consequences of decision making, and ensuring that policies are shaped and utilized to maximize student achievement.

NELP Standard 4 and Connections to *The Framework*

NELP standard 4 for both district-level and building-level leaders lays out the essential aspects of instructional leadership at both levels. First, systems of learning and instruction are specified. These systems include coherent and technologically appropriate curriculum, instruction, and assessment that assure high expectations for all learners throughout the school and district environment (NELP element 4.1 for district-level and building-level leaders).

NELP standard element 4.2 then delves into the district-level leader providing support to principals and other building leaders as they build the instructional capacities of teachers and staff members, while element 4.2 for building-level leaders enhances this instructional capacity within the areas of child development, learning theory, and effective pedagogy (NELP element 4.2 for district-level and building-level leaders).

Elements 4.3 and 4.4 for district-level leaders speaks to the methods that effective district-level leaders use to provide for the professional development of principals and to assure high-quality principal professional practices through effective supervision, evaluation, and feedback. Elements 4.3 and 4.4 for building-level leaders focuses on the employment of effective and appropriate systems of assessment and data analysis focused on the improvement of student instruction. Furthermore, these elements at the building level specify the need for effective staffing, high-quality professional development, and appropriate building-level management practices to support the learning of ALL students.

NELP standard 4 is aligned with multiple areas of *The Framework for Effective Teacher Leadership*. To begin, component 1c recognizes that effective teacher leaders attain student success in the classroom by applying best practices to student learning, utilizing an expansive knowledge base of curricula and pedagogy, and drawing on knowledge of the learner's cultural and community context to assure student success.

Domain 2 speaks to the professional growth of themselves and others through innovative thinking, risk-taking, flexibility, communication, and distributed leadership. It also speaks to technological innovation, effective collaborative practices that build the capacity of others, incorporating policy expectations into instructional practices, and encouraging inquiry and research.

In addition, domain 3, which is the *instructional leadership* piece of *The Framework for Effective Teacher Leadership*, emphasizes the importance of the effective use of assessments, implementing and supporting data-informed practices, providing an effective instructional program, and demonstrating purposeful instructional planning.

NELP Standard 5 and Connections to *The Framework*

NELP district-level and building-level standard 5 specifies the key aspects of community and external leadership that are practiced by effective educational leaders. At the district level, element 5.1 speaks to community engagement that requires the district-level leader to appropriately and meaningfully engage families, community members, and others from both the private and public sectors.

At the building level, element 5.2 speaks to the engagement of the school, families, and community stakeholders in enhancing student success and achievement both in and out of school. In addition, element 5.2 at the district level and element 5.3 at the building level specifies that both district and building leaders must build productive partnerships throughout the learning environment and with all stakeholders. Furthermore, effective two-way communication methods are recognized as essential aspects of successful district and building leadership practices (NELP element 5.3 for district-level leaders and NELP element 5.1 for building-level leaders).

Finally, element 5.4 of the NELP district-level leader standards identifies the district-level leader as the key representative who engages with stakeholders in order to build a shared understanding of and appreciation for decisions that are made in the best interest of student learning and achievement. Element 5.4 of the NELP building-level leader standards identifies the building-level leader as a key advocate for the learning needs and priorities of the school, the district, and the community at large.

Alignment between NELP standard 5 and *The Framework for Effective Teacher Leadership* can be found within component 1b of domain 1, *critical competencies*. This component emphasizes the importance of engaging all stakeholders. Specifically, effective teacher leaders build community by intentionally reaching out to disengaged and/or disenfranchised populations.

Furthermore, they provide outreach and collaboration with families and communities in response to their needs, they respond to the needs and accomplishments of school stakeholders, and they examine problems from multiple perspectives through the connection of ideas. There is also alignment between standard 5 and component 4c, *supports local initiatives*. This component calls on teacher leaders to support the change process, model accountability and responsibility for others, and to collaborate with stakeholders to ensure student growth and the advancement of the profession.

NELP Standard 6 and Connections to *The Framework*

Effective operations and management of people, processes, and data are specified within NELP district-level and building-level standard 6. Element 6.1 within the standards speaks to the management of systems that ensure student learning needs are met fully and appropriately. Element 6.2 within the standards defines the management of fiscal, technological, and other resources that support student learning and that meet the needs of the educational community.

At the district level, element 6.3 addresses the human resources responsibilities of district-level leaders, including hiring, supervision, retention, and succession planning. At the building level, element 6.3 sets forth the importance of effective communication systems within the building environment. Finally, at the district level, element 6.4 requires that leaders promote and establish effective policies and procedures which assure that student and staff welfare and safety remains the highest priority throughout the district. At the building level, element 6.4 addresses the necessity of legal compliance in all aspects of building operations and procedures.

The practices set forth for leaders in NELP standard 6 can also be found within *The Framework for Effective Teacher Leadership* components 2b and

2c. These components speak to various aspects of management and operations within the school building. These include seeking leadership roles that extend beyond the classroom; leading innovation and transformation in the areas of advocacy, management, teaching, and learning; using policy to plan and facilitate professional learning; and engaging, supporting, and facilitating the growth and development of future leaders.

Furthermore, component 4a speaks to teacher leaders practicing resourcefulness by advocating for what is needed to ensure student academic achievement. Finally, component 4c outlines that effective teacher leaders support change by collaborating with stakeholders to ensure learner growth.

NELP Standard 7 and Connections to *The Framework*

Standard 7 within the NELP district-level and building-level standards is the only standard area in which the elements differ substantially from one another. At the district level, standard 7 addresses policy, governance, and advocacy. Specifically, the five elements within this standard at the district level speak to maintaining effective board relations, assuring functional district governance, demonstrating consistent and unwavering legal compliance and policy engagement, and practicing effective advocacy for the students and the district as a whole.

At the building level, standard 7 addresses human resource leadership, including the following areas: effective human resource management, positive professional culture, ideal workplace conditions, and appropriate supervision and evaluation practices.

While the focus of standard 7 differs slightly when comparing the district-level NELP standard 7 to the building-level NELP standard 7, both of these standard areas can be found within *The Framework*. Components 4a, 4b, and 4c of *The Framework* are clearly aligned with NELP standard 7.

These components call on teacher leaders to practice and refine resourcefulness through both appropriate human resources practices and effective and continuous advocacy. They also specify that effective teacher leaders should both model and respond to educational policy in such a way that student growth and learning is maximized. Finally, they specify that teacher leaders engage with and support local initiatives that advance the profession.

Finally, because the NELP standards focus on the preparation of educational leaders at both the district level and the building level, standard 8 specifies internship and clinical practices that must be built in to leadership preparation programs in order to ensure aspiring leaders exit these programs well-prepared to take on the varied and wide-ranging expectations of building-level or district-level leaders.

PSEL LEADERSHIP STANDARDS AND CONNECTIONS TO *THE FRAMEWORK*

According to NPBEA, "The Professional Standards for Educational Leaders (PSEL) are model professional standards that communicate expectations to practitioners, supporting institutions, professional associations, policy makers and the public about the work, qualities and values of effective educational leaders. They will be used by state boards of education to help guide their licensure and professional development programs" (National Policy Board for Educational Administration 2015, 4).

The PSEL standards were set forth in 2015 after a three-year study of the transforming educational leadership environment. This study included reviewing relevant research and seeking the input of researchers, as well as school and district leaders, to identify gaps in prior leadership standards that were subsequently addressed within the PSEL standards (National Policy Board for Educational Administration).

As noted above, the PSEL standards align closely with the NELP district-level and building-level leadership standards. The difference lies in the use of each set of standards. NELP standards are used to articulate what a beginning district-level or building-level administrator should know and be able to do in order to successfully step into a leadership role. Thus, they are most often used to guide the design and implementation of leadership-preparation programs.

PSEL standards, on the other hand, "are model professional standards that communicate expectations to practitioners, supporting institutions, professional associations, policy makers and the public about the work, qualities and values of effective educational leaders. They will be used by state boards of education to help guide their licensure and professional development programs" (National Policy Board for Educational Administration 2015, para. 5). Table 2.1 articulates the alignment between the NELP standards, PSEL standards, and *The Framework*.

TEACHER LEADER MODEL STANDARDS AND CONNECTIONS TO *THE FRAMEWORK*

The TLMS were set forth in 2008 by the Teacher Leader Exploratory Consortium. The consortium is comprised of a diverse group of educational stakeholders including state educational agencies, educational organizations, superintendents, principals, teacher leaders, and representatives from institutions of higher education (Teacher Leader Exploratory Consortium 2008).

Table 2.1. Crosswalk of NELP, PSEL, and FETL

NELP STANDARDS (2018) (District Level/ Building Level)	*PSEL STANDARDS (2015)*	The Framework for Effective Teacher Leadership
1. Mission, Vision, and Core Values	1. Mission, Vision, and Core Values 10. School Improvement	• Component 1a and d • Component 2b and c • Component 3a, b, c, and d • Component 4c
2. Ethics and Professionalism/ Professional Norms	2. Ethics and Professional Norms* 3. Equity and Cultural Responsiveness*	• Component 1d • Component 2b • Component 4c
3. Equity and Cultural Leadership	2. Ethics and Professional Norms* 3. Equity and Cultural Responsiveness*	• Component 3a, c, and d • Component 4b
4. Instructional Leadership	4. Curriculum, Instruction, and Assessment 5. Community of Care and Support for Students* 6. Professional Capacity of School Personnel* 7. Professional Community for Teachers and Staff*	• Component 1c • Component 2a, b, and c • Component 3a, b, c, and d
5. Community and External Leadership	8. Meaningful Engagement of Families and Community*	• Component 1b • Component 4c
6. Management of People, Data, and Processes/Operations and Management	5. Community of Care and Support for Students* 6. Professional Capacity of School Personnel* 9. Operations and Management*	• Component 2b and c • Component 4a, b, and c
7. Policy, Governance, and Advocacy/ Human Resource Leadership	3. Equity and Cultural Responsiveness* 8. Meaningful Engagement of Families and Community* 9. Operations and Management*	• Component 4a, b, and c
8. Internship and Clinical Practice		

The consortium was created in order to examine both the current research and thinking about the critical role of teacher leaders in assuring student growth and achievement.

According to the National Network of State Teachers of the Year (2017), the rationale for this work rested on the belief that "teacher leadership is a potentially powerful strategy to promote effective, collaborative teaching practices in schools that lead to increased student achievement, improved decision making at the school and district level, and create a dynamic teaching profession for the 21st century."

The standards are to be used to facilitate conversations amongst all educational stakeholders about the key components of effective teacher leadership (Teacher Leader Exploratory Consortium 2008). The standards are also used to develop professional learning opportunities, curriculum, and standards for school districts, states, institutions of higher education, and professional organizations. The TLMS were also used as a resource in developing *The Framework*.

The TLMS were mapped to the Interstate School Leaders Licensure Consortium (ISLLC) state standards for school leaders in order to examine alignment between these two sets of leadership standards (Teacher Leader Exploratory Consortium 2008). Furthermore, they are structured similarly to the ISLLC standards in that there are seven domains that comprise broadly stated expectations defining the critical aspects of teacher leadership.

Within each domain, there are related functions that more explicitly define the expectations of teacher leaders within each domain topical area (Teacher Leader Exploratory Consortium 2008). The following sections will provide an overview of each of the seven domains of the TLMS and will also detail the connections to *The Framework*.

TLMS Domain 1 and Connections to *The Framework*

The first domain of the TLMS speaks to the type of collaborative culture that should be nurtured by effective teacher leaders in order to support educator development and student learning (Teacher Leader Exploratory Consortium 2008). The domain specifies that these collaborative environments must incorporate the essential qualities of collegiality, trust, and respect, with an unwavering focus on instruction and student learning. This type of collaborative culture promotes shared decision making and meaningful change.

Within this domain, the effective teacher leader models listening skills, mediating, and facilitating professional discussions. Furthermore, effective teacher leaders honor diverse perspectives by creating an inclusive culture. These teacher leaders use their "knowledge and understanding of different backgrounds, ethnicities, cultures, and languages to promote effective interactions among colleagues" (Teacher Leader Exploratory Consortium 2008, 14).

The functions within this domain of the TLMS are also evident within *The Framework.* Within domain 1 of *The Framework, critical competencies,* component 1a specifies that effective teacher leaders value and draw upon the culture and communities where they serve.

In addition, component 1b calls on teacher leaders to engage all stakeholders by building learning communities that reach out to disenfranchised and disengaged populations. They also connect ideas through the examination of issues from multiple perspectives. Component 1d of *The Framework* also sets forth that effective teacher leaders model high-impact coaching skills by establishing an environment of trust, confidentiality, and respect.

TLMS Domain 2 and Connections to *The Framework*

The second domain of the TLMS specifies that effective teacher leaders access and use research in order to improve professional practices and enhance student learning (Teacher Leader Exploratory Consortium 2008). Teacher leaders also promote the analysis of student data in order to implement enhanced classroom practices that will have a positive impact on student learning. In addition, these leaders facilitate collegial collaboration between K–12 educators and their higher-education counterparts.

The Framework also addresses these key aspects of teacher leadership. For example, component 2b includes an element which specifies that teacher leaders practice and encourage inquiry, research, and sharing information. In addition, component 3d sets forth that effective teacher leaders access, use, and/or engage in research to support and advance instruction.

Furthermore, component 3b specifies that effective teacher leaders implement and support data-informed practices, and component 3c speaks to providing an effective instructional program through the analysis of student data and the implementation of effective instructional practices based on student needs.

TLMS Domain 3 and Connections to *The Framework*

Domain 3 of the TLMS addresses the hallmark of teacher leadership: facilitating professional learning for continuous improvement. This domain states, "The teacher leader understands the evolving nature of teaching and learning, established and emerging technologies, and the school community."

The teacher leader uses this knowledge to "promote, design, and facilitate job-embedded professional learning aligned with school improvement goals" (Teacher Leader Exploratory Consortium 2008, 16). Specifically, effective teacher leaders collaborate to plan job-embedded and sustained professional learning experiences that are aligned with content standards and address school and district improvement goals.

The functions included within domain 3 of the TLMS are embedded throughout domain 2 (*professional growth of self and others*) of *The Framework.* For example, component 2a speaks to the leadership characteristics that are essential for teacher leaders. These characteristics include taking risks, thinking innovatively, modeling flexibility, establishing nonjudgmental relationships, and developing the capacity for distributed leadership.

Furthermore, component 2b sets forth that teacher leaders seek out leadership roles that extend beyond the classroom by leading technological innovation and transformation. Component 2c calls on teacher leaders to also engage and support the development of future leaders by providing support to others that builds competence, confidence, and capacity.

TLMS Domain 4 and Connections to *The Framework*

The fourth domain of the TLMS gets to the heart of the educational process, and speaks to the teacher leader's ability to facilitate improvements in instruction and student learning (Teacher Leader Exploratory Consortium 2008). This is accomplished by using their deep knowledge base to grow the skills of their fellow educators. Effective teacher leaders also model reflective practices and life-long learning. Furthermore, they work collaboratively to assure that school and curricular improvements are aligned to the school's vision, mission, and goals.

This domain aligns very closely with multiple areas of *The Framework.* First, component 1c speaks to attaining student success in the classroom by modeling best practices, drawing on appropriate pedagogy, and infusing an understanding of students' cultural and community contexts into curricula. Second, domain 3 of *The Framework* outlines critical aspects of instructional leadership for teacher leaders. These include the following:

- Effective use of assessments
    - Collecting and reporting evidence of student learning
    - Understanding and using multiple methods of assessment for planning and assessment
    - Assisting with compliance and reporting
- Effective instructional program
    - Collaborating with administration to provide teachers time, support, and training necessary to create and administer assessments; collect, analyze, reflect on, and report data; and set goals
    - Adapting practice to meet the needs of each learner and improve student learning

  - Advocating for instruction that supports the needs of all learners
  - Harnessing the skills, expertise, and knowledge of colleagues to address curricular expectations and student learning needs
- Purposeful planning
  - Promoting instruction that supports every student meeting rigorous learning goals and outcomes
  - Infusing relevant technology to enrich curriculum and instruction
  - Applying developmental, learning, and motivational theories to learning (cognitive, linguistic, social, emotional, and physical)
  - Focusing on student learning specific to classroom management, content, instruction, and assessment
  - Accessing, using, and/or engaging in research to support and advance instruction

Domain 4 (*advocacy*) of *The Framework* also aligns with domain 4 of the TLMS. The components within this domain include practicing and refining resourcefulness, demonstrating an understanding of educational policy, and supporting local initiatives.

TLMS Domain 5 and Connections to *The Framework*

The TLMS domain 5 speaks to promoting the use of assessments and data to ensure school and district improvement. Effective teacher leaders are recognized as being able to create and utilize appropriate formative and summative assessments, and they share this knowledge with their colleagues in order to enhance learning for all students. Furthermore, this TLMS domain delineates that effective teacher leaders use assessment and other data to make decisions that support continuous improvement efforts in classrooms and schools.

This domain aligns to component 3a, which also discusses effective use of assessments by teacher leaders. This component lays out best practices for teacher leaders in collecting, reporting, and analyzing assessments and other data in order to have a positive impact on student learning. In addition, component 3b speaks to how effective teacher leaders implement and support these data-informed practices. In particular, these practices include appropriately designing, implementing, and evaluating student data, as well as designing rigorous learning experiences that are put into place in response to data analysis.

TLMS Domain 6 and Connections to *The Framework*

TLMS domain 6 details how teacher leaders can improve outreach and collaboration with families in community. They explain, "The teacher leader understands that families, cultures, and communities have a significant impact on educational processes and student learning. The teacher leader works with colleagues to promote ongoing systematic collaboration with families, community members, business and community leaders, and other stakeholders to improve the educational system and expand opportunities for student learning" (Teacher Leader Exploratory Consortium 2008).

Furthermore, effective teacher leaders push their colleagues to conduct a self-analysis of their personal understandings of community culture and diversity. They assist colleagues in devising culturally responsive methodologies that have a positive impact on learner success.

This domain aligns with component 1b of *The Framework*, which addresses how effective teacher leaders engage all stakeholders. They do so by engaging disenfranchised populations, by providing outreach to families and the community at large, by responding to the needs of all stakeholders, and by examining all school issues through multiple lenses.

Domain 6 of the TLMS also aligns with domain 4a of *The Framework*, which speaks to the practice and refinement of resourcefulness. Specifically, effective teacher leaders mobilize community resources to support student achievement, solve problems, and achieve goals. In addition, they utilize school, community, and social services resources effectively, and they advocate for all resources that are needed to meet the needs of all learners within the school environment.

TLMS Domain 7 and Connections to *The Framework*

The final domain of the TLMS outlines how effective teacher leaders go about advocating for student learning and the profession (Teacher Leader Exploratory Consortium 2008). These educators understand the mechanics of local, state, and national policy, as well as the roles of educational stakeholders, including school leaders, boards of education, and policy makers.

They utilize this knowledge base in order to advocate for student learning needs and for student-centered practices and decision making. The effective teacher leader "serves as an individual of influence and respect within the school, community, and profession" (Teacher Leader Exploratory Consortium 2008, 20).

This TLMS domain aligns to domain 4 (*advocacy*) within *The Framework*. This domain outlines the following teacher leader practices:

- Practices and refines resourcefulness
  - Mobilizes community resources to support student achievement, solve problems, and achieve goals

  - Uses school and community resources, and social service agencies effectively
  - Advocates for resources (financial, human, material, professional development, training, and time) to meet the needs of all learners
- Demonstrates understanding of educational policy
  - Understands, responds to, and influences the larger political, social, economic, legal, and cultural context
  - Considers and evaluates the potential moral and legal consequences of decision making
  - Builds bridges with administration and stakeholders to advance policies that influence quality instruction and student achievement
  - Steps up and out of classroom to serve at school, district, state, or national levels to shape and implement policy
- Supports local initiatives
  - Creates and supports organizational change
  - Models accountability and responsibility
  - Collaborates with stakeholders to ensure learner growth and advancement of the profession
  - Adheres with fidelity to the evaluation process in accordance with role(s)

SUMMARY

The purpose of this chapter is to provide a detailed explanation as to how national standards for leadership connect to *The Framework for Effective Teacher Leadership.* The NELP district-level and building-level standards were unpacked and alignment with *The Framework* was clarified.

In addition, the PSEL were examined and the areas of alignment to *The Framework* were also thoroughly discussed. Finally, the TLMS were reviewed alongside *The Framework* domains, components, and elements in order to reveal areas of alignment.

Teacher leadership is not a destination, but a journey. It is one in which the continuously developing leader acquires skills and competencies throughout the duration of his or her career. Thus, the competencies set forth within the NELP, PSEL, and TLMS standards, as well as within *The Framework for Effective Teacher Leadership*, can be used as a guidebook along the way. In this manner, the teacher leader continuously grows and develops, never losing sight of the needs of the students and colleagues whom he or she serves.

SELF-ASSESSMENT AND REFLECTION

The leadership standards and *The Framework for Effective Teacher Leadership* can and should be used to assess the skill acquisition of teacher leaders. They are used to assess the effectiveness of current teacher leader practice, to set goals for future growth and improvement, and for program preparation and development. Choose one set of standards presented in this chapter and conduct a self-assessment based on the standard descriptors. Identify one area of strength and one area for growth for yourself as a teacher leader. Set a goal to address the growth area.

REFERENCES

National Policy Board for Educational Administration. (2015). Alliance for school leadership. Retrieved from http://npbea.org/

———. (2015). NPBEA history. Retrieved from http://npbea.org/about-npbea/npbea-history/

———. (2018). National Educational Leadership Preparation 2018. Reston, VA: Author.

———. (2015). Professional Standards for Educational Leaders 2015. Reston, VA: Author.

National Network of State Teachers of the Year. (2017). Teacher leader model standards. Retrieved from http://www.nnstoy.org/teacher-leader-model-standards/

Teacher Leadership Exploratory Consortium. (2008). Teacher leader model standards. Retrieved from http://www.nnstoy.org/download/standards/Teacher%20Leader%20Standards.pdf

University Council for Educational Administration. (1987). *Leaders for America's schools: The report of the National Commission on Excellence in Educational Administration.* Tempe, AZ: Daniel E. Griffiths.

Chapter Three

The Diversity of Teacher Leaders

OBJECTIVES

Throughout this chapter you will:

1. Explore district-level and building-level roles (NELP 1, 2, 3, 4, 5 ,6, 7; PSEL 1, 2, 3, 4, 5, 6, 7, 8, 9, 10; TLMS 1, 2, 3, 4, 5, 6, 7; NBPTS 1, 2, 3, 5).
2. Examine criterion for selection (NELP 1, 2, 3, 4, 5 ,6, 7; PSEL 1, 2, 3, 4, 5, 6, 7, 8, 9, 10; TLMS 1, 2, 3, 4, 5, 6, 7; NBPTS 1, 2, 3).
3. Investigate preparation for responsibilities (NELP 1, 2, 3, 4, 5 ,6, 7; PSEL 1, 2, 3, 4, 5, 6, 7, 8, 9, 10; TLMS 1, 2, 3, 4, 5, 6, 7; NBPTS 1, 2 3).
4. Investigate recognition and support of administration (NELP 1, 2, 3, 4, 5, 6, 7; PSEL 1, 2, 3, 4, 5, 6, 7, 8, 9, 10; TLMS 1, 2, 3, 4, 5, 6, 7).
5. Investigate recognition by state agencies (NELP 1, 2, 3, 4,5 ,6, 7; PSEL 1, 2, 3, 4, 5, 6, 7, 8, 9, 10; TLMS 1, 2, 3, 4, 5, 6, 7).

The roles and responsibilities that teacher leaders fulfill are diverse and complex. There is a significant variance among schools, districts, states, and on a national level as to how the role is viewed and used on a daily basis. Furthermore, the role tends to evolve as other leadership roles at both the building and district level change.

Responsibilities and expectations are determined based upon needs that are in a constant state of flux in the field of education. Thus, any attempt to define the roles and responsibilities of teacher leaders must assure a broad interpretation that does not exclude or minimize any aspect of teacher leadership. In this chapter, we provide a broad overview of current teacher-leadership roles and examine the varied aspects of teacher leadership preparation, recognition, and support at the building, district, and state levels.

DISTRICT-LEVEL AND BUILDING-LEVEL ROLES

The Massachusetts Department of Education assembled a Professional Learning Network during the 2014–2015 school year in order to examine teacher leadership. The network's intention was to name both the roadblocks and methods to overcome these roadblocks in order to assist schools and districts in more effectively utilizing teacher leaders (Massachusetts Department of Elementary and Secondary Education 2015a).

When examining the definition of roles, the network set forth several suggestions for districts and buildings. First, it recommended that districts and schools assure that the scope of the role is manageable so that teacher leaders have plenty of time to devote to their own classrooms, as well as leading their colleagues in improvement initiatives.

In addition, they cautioned that care must be taken in balancing the specificity of the role versus the flexibility that is needed to differentiate according to building and district needs. Furthermore, details in regard to the time needed to fulfill role expectations as well as the anticipated structure of the role are key pieces that must be communicated at the outset.

In addition, prospective teacher leaders must have supports such as professional development and time for collegial communication and collaboration, and these supports must also be clearly communicated prior to entering the role. Finally, clarity as to the term of service is key, as some positions may change or terminate after a specified period of time.

Harrison and Killion (2007) set forth ten roles for teacher leaders that can be used at the building and/or district levels to contribute to overall school- and district-wide continuous improvement. These ten roles and an explanation of each are as follows:

1. Resource Provider—Teacher leaders might provide resources to both their colleagues and building- and district-level leaders. These resources vary from creative uses for technology and multimedia to effective curricular practices and materials to research-based instructional practices that meet varied learning needs.
2. Instructional Specialist—Teacher leaders might not only provide resources for instruction, but they might also model effective instructional

practices and/or observe colleagues with the intention of providing individualized support based on specific needed areas of educator professional growth.

3. Curriculum Specialist—Teacher leaders often possess a depth of knowledge in one or more curricular areas that is beneficial to school and district-level staff as they work to meet student learning needs. This might include a core area such as math or reading, or it might encompass a particular methodology, such as guided reading, flexible grouping, providing behavioral supports, or using technology to support students' unique learning needs.
4. Classroom Supporter—No matter what the area of expertise, teacher leaders have a deep knowledge base of what works in the classroom, and they provide support to their colleagues as they implement effective strategies to meet student needs. This includes frequent observation and feedback, recommendations as to the ideal physical and curricular structures for various classroom settings, coteaching with colleagues, and/or modeling new teaching strategies and practices for others.
5. Learning Facilitator—Naturally, teacher leaders are focused on advancing student learning, but effective teacher leaders also extend this focus to include other colleagues, as well as building- and district-level leaders. The teacher leader may serve as a building-wide or district-wide instructional or technology coach, and, as such, may frequently plan professional learning opportunities to facilitate the learning and professional growth of others. Furthermore, the teacher leader bridges the gap between the educational research base and a practitioner's understanding of best practices. Thus, the effective teacher leader can navigate and pare down research so that it is both understandable and accessible to his or her colleagues.
6. Mentor—The role of mentoring is often key to the roles and responsibilities that are assigned to teacher leaders. This mentorship might involve being formally assigned to a new teacher as a part of the teacher induction process, but it might also encompass working with more experienced teachers who need to refine or enhance their practices or those who have transferred to a new grade level or content area. This method of leading from the classroom contributes to, develops, and enhances the types of collaborative practices that can have a positive impact on teacher retention and improved outcomes for students.
7. School Leader—Teacher leaders are often called upon to serve in formal roles as part of building- and district-level teams, committees, and learning communities. The work of these groups focuses around all aspects of

school and district improvement. These teams or committees oversee and provide support and direction for all aspects of classroom, school, and district-wide practices, including, but not limited to, the topics of curriculum, instruction, assessment, behavioral support, school operations and safety, and school and district policies and procedures.

8. Data Coach—Teacher leaders provide support in planning and enacting responsive action based on data collected at the classroom, school, district, state, and national levels. These leaders understand and can articulate effective ways to use data to inform instruction, as well as providing support in the collection and interpretation of data on a continuous basis. Finally, teacher leaders are adept at looking beyond the data to recognize additional nonquantifiable student conditions and needs that also require the attention and response from effective educators in order for student learning to take place.
9. Catalyst for Change—When asked how to change the culture and capacity of a school district, Charlotte Danielson (as quoted in Griffin [2013, 29]), explained the following:

   > It's an instructional leadership issue and a professional development issue. It involves professional learning and conversations with site administrators and teachers. The more conversation the better. Site administrators as instructional leaders must appreciate the role of school culture, a professional culture, a culture of professional inquiry. They must define teaching as not just what you do with your kids for six hours a day but also about building a professional culture in which everybody is still learning.

10. Learner—The teacher leader's mindset is that of a lifelong learner. The only aspect of his or her professional practices that remain constant are the continual evolution and refinement of those practices. Thus, the teacher leader models the role of lead learner for students, for colleagues, and for building- and district-level leaders. And it is through the modeling of lifelong learning that the teacher leader positively impacts all aspects of the educational environment—it is that commitment to improvement that permeates and becomes the lifeblood of a healthy and vibrant learning community.

Teacher leaders are key stakeholders in inspiring the healthy culture and level of professional inquiry that promotes and supports ongoing change and improvement in all aspects of the school environment. By modeling and supporting continuous forward movement, fellow educators view teacher leaders as role models in how to change practices to better support every area of student instruction and support.

CRITERION FOR SELECTION

Von Frank (2011, p. 1) stated that effective teachers' and teacher leaders' roles are different. She explained, "Some educators believe that many teachers may learn to be highly effective, but not all want to or will be teacher leaders. Others contend that all teachers should acquire the skills of teacher leaders." Table 3.1 reflects Von Frank's differences between effective teachers and teacher leaders.

Carr (2013) advocates for the usage of the seven domains of the Teacher Leader Model Standards (TLMS) as the criteria for selecting effective teacher leaders. As discussed in detail in chapter 2, these seven domains are also reflected in *The Framework for Effective Teacher Leadership* and include the following:

- Domain I: Fostering a Collaborative Culture to Support Educator Development and Student Learning
- Domain II: Accessing and Using Research to Improve Practice and Student Learning

Table 3.1. VonFrank's differences between effective teachers and teacher leaders

Effective teachers . . .	*Teacher leaders . . .*
Are aware of professional research and literature	Are engaged in professional research and are willing to engage with others
Can explain and analyze their own practice	Lead instructional change
Are change agents	Are change agents and negotiators of change
Are members of and initiate communities of learners	Build capacity in colleagues and systems
Build mutual trust and respect in the classroom	Know how to facilitate and support adult learning
Create safe, positive learning environments	Are as effective with adults as with students
Understand individual student needs and engage in culturally responsive instruction	Think "we" instead of "I"; for example, "What can we do to make this better?"
Analyze data to impact student learning	Teach beyond the classroom; they focus on advancing the profession and lead change
Share expertise	Are boundary spanners
Engage in creative insubordination	Are opportunistic; see and seize opportunities
Belong to professional organizations	Lead by example

Source: Von Frank (2011)

- Domain III: Promoting Professional Learning for Continuous Improvement
- Domain IV: Facilitating Improvements in Instruction and Student Learning
- Domain V: Promoting the Use of Assessments and Data for School and District Improvement
- Domain VI: Improving Outreach and Collaboration with Families and Community
- Domain VII: Advocating for Student Learning and the Profession (Teacher Leadership Exploratory Consortium 2008).

Thus, those who are seeking effective teacher leaders can evaluate the level of expertise of candidates within each of the TLMS domains in order to determine their overall capacity to fulfill various teacher leadership roles.

Beyond utilizing the standards as criteria for selecting effective teacher leaders, Carr (2013) also advocates for those hiring teacher leaders to look at the actual responsibilities that are key to the role (instructional coach, professional development specialist, curriculum designer, assessment expert, etc.) for which they are hiring in order to further specify essential skill sets.

Finally, those hiring teacher leaders must delineate and seek out the specific knowledge base that is required for the successful implementation of school and district-wide efforts and initiatives. Carr (2013, p. 2) explained, "Together, these three areas—standards, role, and implementation—guide identification of the criteria for selection of teacher leaders."

Jackson et al. (2010) also defined specific criterion of effective teacher leaders. Rather than discuss pedagogical skills, they described six constructs under which sets of skills could be organized to create a framework that accurately names the essential personal skills of effective teacher leaders. Their eight constructs and the associated skills identified by Jackson et al. (2010) are shown below:

- Work ethic
- Achievement oriented
  - Commitment
  - Persistence
  - Resourcefulness
  - Responsible
- Teamwork
  - Agreeableness
  - Collaboration
  - Communication
  - Conflict resolution

- Leadership
  - Influence
  - Leadership preparedness
- Openness
  - Adaptability
  - Creativity
  - Open-minded
- Vision
- Positive affect
- Risk-taking
- Teaching-related skills
  - Attitude
  - Pedagogical knowledge (Jackson et al. 2010, 18)

PREPARATION FOR RESPONSIBILITIES

Teacher leadership preparation is just as varied as the roles in which teacher leaders serve, ranging from formal university training and/or formal professional development opportunities to informal training through diverse experiences and collaborative opportunities. Greenlee (2007, 9) explained that

> traditionally, teachers who want to remain in the classroom and pursue graduate degrees enroll in curriculum and instruction programs, while those who want to be school principals enroll in educational leadership programs.
>
> However, many of the participants in educational leadership programs wish to assume more active roles in education reform and school renewal as teacher leaders without moving to administration.

In 2004, York-Barr and Duke specified the varied ways in which teacher leaders are prepared for their roles. They cited evidence of the need for formalized training of teacher leaders and pushed back against the assumption that aspiring teacher leaders intuitively know how to take up the mantle of leadership. Thus, they called for expanded formalized programming intentionally designed to prepare teacher leaders for the unique roles they fulfill.

In 2016, Wixom reported that,

> Some states have created policies to formalize the teacher leader process in policy. As of 2013, three states had a master teacher designation, eight states had some type of certification endorsements for teacher leaders, 20 states had tiers for advanced or master teachers within their multi-tiered certification systems and four states had introduced teacher leader roles to assist teachers with the Common Core State Standards transition (p. 2).

This diversity in state recognition and use of teacher leaders is reflected in the diversity of preparation methods, both formal and informal. It speaks to the need for *The Framework for Effective Teacher Leadership* that is the subject of this book. *The Framework* can be used to delineate the expected outcomes and competencies of effective teacher leaders, and as such, *The Framework* can also be used in the planning and execution of effective formal and informal preparation programs.

RECOGNITION AND SUPPORT OF ADMINISTRATION

The Massachusetts Department of Elementary and Secondary Education (2015a) identified specific characteristics of a school culture that supports teacher leadership. Building and district officials must be keenly aware of each aspect of this healthy school culture and must nurture it on a continuous basis in order to also effectively nurture teacher leadership.

The first essential characteristic is the development of a collegial environment in which teacher collaboration is purposefully planned for and takes place on a regular basis, both formally and informally. Furthermore, all educational stakeholders within this environment should be able to articulate a clear vision for the school environment, as well as the school's goals in working toward realizing the vision.

Also, the department called for a problem-solving orientation within the school environment. This means that the staff is more engaged in finding solutions than identifying and ruminating over problems. In addition, "Students are ours, as opposed to yours/mine. The students' successes and challenges belong to everyone, and everyone is committed to making improvements" (Massachusetts Department of Elementary and Secondary Education 2015a, 3).

A high level of trust is another key aspect of school culture that promotes and supports teacher leadership (Massachusetts Department of Elementary and Secondary Education 2015a). In environments where trust is present, teachers are unafraid to accurately and fully name problems, concerns, and setbacks in order to move forward toward successful solutions. In an environment of trust, all educators are willing to make themselves vulnerable to one another. As a result, all stakeholders are focused on professional growth and improvement and can freely learn from mistakes and missteps.

Finally, according to the department, building and district leaders ensure there is clear communication in a healthy school culture where teacher leadership can flourish. As a result, everyone is on the same page and there are no mixed messages being sent or received. The building and district have multiple methods of communication in place in order to model and support these healthy communication strategies.

Furthermore, school leaders' mindsets can contribute to a school environment that promotes teacher leadership (Massachusetts Department of Elementary and Secondary Education 2015a). Specifically, the following is recommended:

- Have a growth mindset about all staff
- Be humble and reflective
- Be a community-builder
- Be approachable and flexible
- Step out of the comfort zone as a leader.

In addition to the above methods for advancing teacher leadership at the building and district level, representatives from nine states recently worked together to create a State Action Framework for Teacher Leadership as a result of recommendations from the Every Student Succeeds Act (ESSA). This framework is a "state-developed step-by-step process and conceptual framework with examples and tools to support the growth of teacher leadership" (Leading Educators 2017, 1). This toolkit lays out three phases for growing teacher leadership:

- Phase 1: Identify rationale and goals
- Phase 2: Choose and implement strategies
- Phase 3: Drive continuous improvement

Furthermore, this toolkit is built from the following perspective:

> Effective teacher leadership marries form with function in order to create transformative change in schools. Teacher leadership initiatives are designed with function when they are designed to advance other pressing priorities supported by relevant data, rather than created for their own sake. Teacher leadership initiatives are designed with form when roles are clearly defined, with sufficient time, support, authority, and resources to be effective. (Leading Educators 2017, 7)

Thus, building and district administrators can support and expand teacher leadership by attending to both the form and function of their initiatives that are put into place to support the growth and development of teacher leaders.

RECOGNITION BY STATE AGENCIES

Just as the roles and responsibilities of teacher leaders vary significantly among schools, districts, and states, so too do the varied means of recognition of teacher leaders from state to state. While some teacher leaders might fulfill a coaching or specialist role with no specific training or certification in one district, other districts may require specific endorsements, certifications, or licenses in order to be deemed qualified for specific teacher leadership roles.

Most often, formal teacher leader endorsements, certifications, and licensure are earned after initial teacher training and induction has taken place and according to state program requirements.

Illinois, for example, identifies three pipelines to teacher leadership (Soglin, Hunt, and Reilly 2016). The first is the role of the school principal for those candidates who may want to "to dip their toes into leadership training in the event that someday they may pursue a principalship" (Soglin, Hunt, and Reilly 2016, p. 6). Because principal preparation in Illinois is so focused on fulfilling the role of the instructional leader, candidates who pursue their principal credentials are also engaged in programming that builds their skills in all aspects of instructional leadership as well.

The second pipeline is to fulfill the role of a school- or district-based teacher leader. This role encompasses all seven domains of the TLMS. According to Soglin, Hunt, and Reilly (2016, p. 6), "Good teachers form the foundation of good schools. Improving teachers' skills and knowledge is one of the most important investments of time and money that local, state, and national leaders can make in education." Teacher leaders traversing this pipeline in Illinois typically pursue the Illinois teacher-leader endorsement.

The final pipeline in Illinois is identified as a classroom-based teacher leader. "Such teachers recognize that students' school experiences involve not only interactions with individual teachers but also complex systems in place throughout the school, district, nation and world. This awareness prompts these teachers to want to influence change" (Soglin, Hunt, and Reilly 2016, p. 6). While leaders emerging from this pipeline may also pursue additional credentialing and endorsement, their focus lies on inspiring change beyond the school walls, reaching into their communities, as well as policy and practice.

In addition, Illinois advocates for micro-credentialing as one way to fulfill the professional development needs of teacher leaders. Micro-credentialing is also encouraged by The National Network of State Teachers of the Year (NNSTOY) organization. Soglin, Hunt, and Reilly (2016, p. 27) stated the following in regard to micro-credentialing:

> Micro-credentialing offers the opportunity to shift from the credit hour and continuing-education requirements that dominate professional development to a system based on evidence of progress in specific instructional skills. Through micro-credentialing, professional development becomes more relevant, personalized, and engaging. Teachers engaged in a micro-credentialing

process have to show application of the learning process and its impact in their classrooms or schools.

Ohio offers a post-master's teacher leadership endorsement; however, many aspiring teacher leaders opt to earn Ohio principal licensure, which can be embedded within a master's program. Furthermore, many Ohio districts utilize the principal licensure as a qualification for roles that could conceivably be viewed as teacher leadership positions (curriculum coordinator, instructional coach, technology coach, etc.). Ohio recognizes and affirms teacher leadership through the following programs and initiatives:

- Teacher Leader Endorsement
- Four-Tier Licensure System (Senior and Lead Professional Educator Licenses)
- 2010 Teacher Incentive Fund Grant
- Resident Educator Mentoring and Exploring Leadership
- Ohio Teacher of the Year
- Milken Educator Award
- Ohio Improvement Process Team Structures (Ohio Department of Education 2017).

In 2017, Ohio also took steps to further advance teacher leadership throughout the state. The Ohio Department of Education collaborated with Ohio teachers and administrators, educator associations, and the Ohio Department of Higher Education to create the Ohio Teacher Leadership Framework. According to the Ohio Department of Education (2017, p. 3), "The Ohio Teacher Leadership Framework seeks to present the central components of teacher leadership in Ohio while also recognizing the diverse forms (both formal and informal) of teacher leadership that already exist in Ohio's schools and districts."

Specifically, this framework identifies five broad components of teacher leadership:

1. Fostering Collaborative Culture,
2. Advancing Instruction and Student Learning,
3. Driving Initiatives,
4. Practicing Equity and Ethics, and
5. Building Relationships and Partnerships (Ohio Department of Education 2017).

The intention of setting forth these five inclusive categories of teacher leadership was to leave the framework open-ended enough that it might accurately reflect the diverse roles in which teacher leaders serve.

SUMMARY

The purpose of this chapter was to explore the diversity of teacher leadership and to investigate the varied roles and responsibilities that teacher leaders fulfill. The vision for teacher leadership is different from school to school, district to district, and state to state. Because of these variances, the criterion for selection of teacher leaders is also quite diverse. Furthermore, preparation for the responsibilities that are encompassed within teacher leadership roles might be offered formally or informally and might encompass graduate-level programming and/or specific types of professional development, as well as opportunities for collaborative practices to take place on a regular basis.

In addition, the more support for teacher leadership that is offered at the building and district level, the greater the likelihood of success. Finally, the diversity of teacher leadership is reflected by the different ways that state agencies address the needs of teacher leaders. Despite the many and varied roles, definitions, and responsibilities of teacher leaders, the one area of agreement is that teacher leadership is a critical aspect of assuring teacher professional growth, thereby positively impacting student academic success.

SELF-ASSESSMENT AND REFLECTION

This chapter presented a number of ways in which the role of the teacher leader is diverse. For example, criterion for selection, teacher leader preparation and responsibilities, types of recognition and support offered by buildings and districts are ways in which teacher leaders are recognized by state agencies. Present solid arguments for both the pros and cons of this broad and diverse interpretation of an educational role. Is it a benefit or drawback to teacher leaders that their roles can be so diverse? Also, address the benefits and drawbacks to students and schools.

REFERENCES

Carr, J. (2013). Selecting and supporting teacher leaders. Retrieved from http://pdo.ascd.org/LMSCourses/PD13OC010M/media/Leading_Prof_Learning_M2_Reading201.pdf

Greenlee, B. J. (2007). Building teacher leadership capacity through educational leadership programs. *Journal of Research for Educational Leaders, 4*(1), 44–74.

Griffin, L., ed. (2013). Charlotte Danielson on teacher evaluation and quality. *School Administrator 1*(70), 27–31.

Harrison, C. and Killion, J. (2007). Ten roles for teacher leaders. *Educational Leadership, 65*(1), 74–77.

Jackson, T., Burrus, J., Bassett, K., and Roberts, R. D. (2010). Teacher leadership: An assessment framework for an emerging area of professional practice. Retrieved from https://www.ets.org/Media/Research/pdf/RR-10-27.pdf

Leading Educators. (2017). State teacher leadership toolkit: Created by states, for states. Retrieved from https://education-first.com/wp-content/uploads/2017/02/Education-First-Leading-Educators-State-Teacher-Leadership-Toolkit-Jan-2017.pdf

Massachusetts Department of Elementary and Secondary Education. (2015a). Building a school culture that supports teacher leadership. Retrieved from http://www.doe.mass.edu/edeval/leadership/BuildingSchoolCulture.pdf

———. (2015b). Creating and sustaining teacher leadership roles: Lessons learned from districts. Retrieved from http://www.doe.mass.edu/edeval/leadership/CreateSustainRoles.pdf

Ohio Department of Education. (2017). Ohio teacher leadership framework. Retrieved from http://education.ohio.gov/getattachment/Topics/Teaching/News/Ohio-Teacher-Leadership-Framework-now-available/Ohio-Teacher-Leader-Framework_508_compliant.pdf.aspx?lang=en-US

Soglin, A., Hunt, E., and Reilly, P. (2016). Teacher leadership report. Retrieved from https://education.illinoisstate.edu/downloads/csep/Wallace%20TL%20Report%20Layout%20FINAL.pdf

Teacher Leadership Exploratory Consortium. (2008). Teacher leader model standards. Retrieved from http://www.nnstoy.org/download/standards/Teacher%20Leader%20Standards.pdf

Von Frank, V. (2011). Teacher leader standards: Consortium seeks to strengthen profession within leadership role. *Learning Forward 6*(5), 1–4.

Wixom, M. (2016). Mitigating teacher shortages: Teacher leadership. Retrieved from https://www.ecs.org/wp-content/uploads/Mitigating-Teacher-Shortages-Teacher-leaders.pdf

York-Barr, J., and Duke, K. (2004, Fall). What do we know about teacher leadership? Findings from two decades of scholarship. *Review of Educational Research, 74*(3), 255–316.

Chapter Four

Setting the Stage for *The Framework for Effective Teacher Leadership*

OBJECTIVES

Throughout this chapter you will:

1. Understand the development of *The Framework for Effective Teacher Leadership* (PSEL 7, 10; NELP 2, 3, 4; NBPTS 1, 2, 3, 4, 5; MTLS 1, 3, 4, 7).
2. Examine the format of *The Framework for Effective Teacher Leadership* (PSEL 7, 10; NELP 2, 3, 4; NBPTS 4, 5; MTLS 2, 4, 5).
3. Investigate the four domains of *The Framework* (PSEL 7, 10; NELP 2, 3, 4; NBPTS 4, 5; MTLS 2, 4, 5).
4. Interpret evidence specific to the Levels of Performance (PSEL 1, 2, 3, 4, 5, 6, 7, 8, 9,10; NELP 1, 2, 3, 4, 5, 6, 7; NBPTS 1, 2, 3, 4, 5; MTLS 1, 3, 4, 7).
5. Recognize the need for *The Framework* (PSEL 7, 10; NELP 2, 3, 4, 5, 6, 7; NBPTS 1, 4, 5; MTLS 1, 3, 4, 7).
6. Discern focus on the practitioner (PSEL 2, 4, 6, 7, 8, 9 10; NELP 2, 3, 4; NBPTS 4, 5; MTLS 1, 3, 4, 7).

DEVELOPMENT OF *THE FRAMEWORK FOR EFFECTIVE TEACHER LEADERSHIP*

"We know that the best way to create ownership is to have those responsible for implementation develop the plan for themselves. . . . It simply doesn't work to ask people to sign on when they haven't been involved in the planning process" (Wheatley 2006, p. 68). *The Framework for Effective Teacher Leadership* was developed over the course of three years, and reflects the voice of teacher, administrators, teacher leaders and those in other roles (see chapter 7).

The framework and rubrics developed align with a number of standards and competencies bridging teaching to leadership through effective teacher leadership. The standards and competencies examined include: Teacher Leader Model Standards (Teacher Leadership Consortium 2008); The Teacher Leadership Competencies (Center for Teaching Quality, National Board for Professional Teaching Standards, and the National Education Association 2014); *Transforming Professional Practice: A Framework for Effective Leadership* (Strike et al. 2016); *Framework for Teaching* (Danielson 2013); ICF coaching; *ELCC* (2011) and *ISLLC* (2015) standards.

When studying these standards and competencies, it becomes clear that there are many commonalities. It is through these standards and competencies that teacher leaders can be supervised, evaluated, coached, mentored, provided opportunity to practice, and anchored in a model that promotes professional learning and growth. *The Framework for Effective Teacher Leadership* was created as a tool to provide continuity.

While proven to have many variances under the umbrella of teacher leader, such as levels of responsibility, roles, models, pay scales, and benefits, *The Framework for Effective Teacher Leadership* provides continuity. Through use of this tool, elements aligned with standards and competencies provide specific guidance helpful in self-reflection of personal strengths and areas in need of improvement to enhance performance and increase results. The four domains of *The Framework for Effective Teacher Leadership* are:

Domain 1—Critical Competencies
Domain 2—Professional Growth of Self and Others
Domain 3—Instructional Leadership
Domain 4—Advocacy

The Framework for Effective Teacher Leadership captures the complexity of leadership and highlights that the skills are interrelated. While not a checklist, *The Framework for Effective Teacher Leadership* provides common traits of those in teacher leadership positions. It offers a means through which teacher leaders can view skills commonly identified in leadership within a context of self-assessment, reflection, identification of goals, and continuous improvement. It also promotes common language for professional dialogue and ongoing professional learning.

The Framework for Effective Teacher Leadership highlights successful, accomplished, and effective professional practice through a lens that identifies and defines what leaders should know (theory) and do (practice). It also allows for the identification of inconsistent performance or areas of need due to lack of experience, expertise, or commitment. *The Framework for Effective Teacher Leadership* can be used in a formative or summative setting. It is the authors' intent to provide the framework for formative evaluation in an effort to promote ongoing professional learning and growth of teacher leaders as they move through the continuum of their careers.

FORMAT OF *THE FRAMEWORK FOR EFFECTIVE TEACHER LEADERSHIP*

The Framework for Effective Teacher Leadership has two main parts: *The Framework* and the rubrics that align with *The Framework.* The rubrics reflect each component within the four domains and are broken down to capture the essential information of the elements within that component. The rubric reflects the levels of performance for each of the elements. For the purpose of this book, the authors have coupled domains 2 and 3, and domains 1 and 4. Each will be reviewed in depth in future chapters.

After reviewing the literature and exploring standards associated with teacher leadership, the authors have structured *The Framework* within four domains that reflect general areas of knowledge. There are fourteen components identified, each describing specific skills within the domain. Each component is broken down to explicit dispositions and practices of effective teacher leaders. There are fifty-six elements identified by the authors. Tables 4.1 and 4.2 provide *The Framework for Effective Teacher Leadership* in its entirety. This allows the reader to see the domains, components, and elements as a whole.

The domains are divided into quadrants. To examine the domains in order, the reader can begin at the top left, move to the top right, then lower right, and finally the bottom left to follow the domains in order of number. Within each domain are numbered components, and under the numbered components are bulleted elements. This allows the reader to move from the general knowledge category, to the subsets of skills in the components, to the elements that reflect the dispositions and practices required.

For example, domain 3—*instructional leadership*, contains four components and seventeen elements. The second component in this domain is "3b. Implements and supports data informed practices." Under this component, the first element is "Assists with design, implementation, evaluation, and analysis of student data." The domain applies to all educators, as all are focused on student learning. The component, while still important to all teacher leaders, is more targeted with regard to the expectations of the person based on his or her

Table 4.1. *The Framework for Effective Teacher Leadership*—Domains 1 and 2

Domain 1: Critical Competencies	*Domain 2: Professional Growth of Self and Others*
1a. Values and draws upon the culture and community one serves • Advances the mission, vision, and goals of the school • Advocates a mindful culture that reflects equity, fairness, and diversity • Initiates cultural responsiveness • Maintains professionalism in all interactions 1b. Engages all stakeholders • Builds community through a concerted collaborative effort to reach out to disenfranchised or disengaged populations • Provides outreach and collaboration with families and community in response to community needs • Responds to needs and accomplishments of stakeholders • Examines problems and issues from multiple perspectives and connects ideas 1c. Attains student success in the classroom • Applies and models best practice to student learning • Utilizes knowledge of content areas, curriculum, cross-disciplinary skills, and pedagogy • Draws on knowledge of the learner's cultural and community context 1d. Models effective coaching skills • Establishes an environment of trust, confidentiality, and respect • Engages in direct and appropriate communication • Establishes a presence to build relationships across professional communities • Provides active listening, alternatives, specific and meaningful feedback, relevant application, and details	2a. Demonstrates Leadership • Supports innovative thinking and risk-taking efforts • Models flexibility and establishes safe, nonjudgmental relationships • Identifies and communicates needs of self and others to advance shared goals and job embedded professional learning • Develops the capacity for distributed leadership and encourages collective wisdom 2b. Initiates and encourages growth in self and others • Seeks appropriate leadership roles and opportunities extending beyond one's classroom • Leads technological innovation and transformation for communication, advocacy, management, networking, learning, and teaching • Uses education, economic, and social trends and policy in planning and facilitating professional learning • Practices and encourages inquiry, research, and sharing information 2c. Engages and supports the development of future leaders • Empowers and engages individuals for success based on a knowledge of strengths, personality, style, practices, and beliefs • Aligns individual's work with intentionality based on goals and interests • Demonstrates interpersonal effectiveness through articulation of ways to support others to build competence, confidence, and capacity • Transforms others through thought-provoking questioning, difficult conversations, and engaging in professional dialogue that uncovers assumptions and beliefs • Builds efficacy through self-management, self-monitoring, and self-modification

Source: ©2015 Strike

Table 4.2. ***The Framework for Effective Teacher Leadership*—Domains 3 and 4**

Domain 4: Advocacy	*Domain 3: Instructional Leadership*
4a. Practices and refines resourcefulness • Mobilizes community resources to support student achievement, solve problems, and achieve goals • Uses school and community resources, and social service agencies effectively • Advocates for resources (financial, human, material, professional development, training, and time) to meet the needs of all learners	3a. Demonstrates effective use of assessments • Collects and reports evidence of student learning • Understands and uses multiple methods of assessment to engage learners in own growth, monitor learner progress, and guide teachers and learners in decision making • Assists with compliance and preparation of local, state, and federal reporting • Increases the capacity of colleagues to effectively use multiple assessment tools based on purpose, use, and reporting of assessment
4b. Demonstrates understanding of educational policy • Understands, responds to, and influences the larger political, social, economic, legal, and cultural context • Considers and evaluates the potential moral and legal consequences of decision making • Builds bridges with administration and stakeholders to advance policies that influence quality instruction and student achievement • Steps up and out of classroom to serve at school, district, state, or national levels to shape and implement policy	3b. Implements and supports data-informed practices • Assists with design, implementation, evaluation, and analysis of student data • Assists in accessing data, reflective analysis, collaborative interpretation of results, and application of findings to improve teaching and learning, and communication of results • Collects and uses data to identify goals and promote learning • Designs individual and rigorous collaborative learning that encourages positive social interaction, active engagement in learning, and self-motivation 3c. Provides an effective instructional program • Collaborates with administration to provide teachers the time, support, and training necessary to create and administer assessments; collect, analyze, reflect on, and report data; and set goals • Adapts practice to meet the needs of each learner and improve student learning • Advocates for instruction that supports the needs of all learners • Harnesses the skills, expertise, and knowledge of colleagues to address curricular expectations and student learning needs
4c. Supports local initiatives • Creates and supports organizational change • Models accountability and responsibility • Collaborates with stakeholders to ensure learner growth and advancement of the profession • Adheres with fidelity to the evaluation process in accordance with role/s	3d. Demonstrates purposeful planning • Plans or collaborates to promote instruction that supports every student meeting rigorous learning goals/outcomes and transference to practice • Infuses relevant technology to enrich curriculum and instruction • Applies developmental, learning, and motivational theories to learning (cognitive, linguistic, social, emotional, and physical) • Focuses on student learning specific to classroom management, content, instruction, and assessment • Accesses, uses, and/or engages in research to support and advance instruction

Source: ©2015 Strike

role. The element conveys the disposition or practice required of the effective teacher leader in order to support students, colleagues and the school or district.

It is important to note that while each of the domains may have a different number of components, or each of the components a different number of elements, each reflects an equally important aspect of effective teacher leadership. Each element is of the same weight as other elements, and each component is of the same weight as other components. *The Framework for Effective Teacher Leadership* includes each concept only once even though they may overlap in day-to-day practices. Finally, the verbs used focus on active performance rather than beliefs, dispositions, or intentions. Actions can be observed and analyzed, and each verb was carefully chosen to align with and highlight the desired action for effective leadership.

THE FOUR DOMAINS OF *THE FRAMEWORK FOR EFFECTIVE TEACHER LEADERSHIP*

Teacher leaders are pulled in many directions throughout the day. There is no job description that could capture all that teacher leaders do, but there are similarities regardless of one's role. These areas are identified in the four domains of *The Framework*: *critical competencies, professional growth of self and others, instructional leadership,* and *advocacy.*

Critical competencies describes the foundational competencies teacher leaders need to lead effectively, and the observable behaviors of effective teacher leaders. The components within this domain create an infrastructure that establishes value and draws upon the culture and community one serves; engages all stakeholders; attains student success in the classroom; and models effective coaching skills. The skills and dispositions within this domain build a solid foundation that reflects shared leadership, requires effective communication, and promotes a positive school culture.

Professional growth of self and others describe competencies an effective teacher leader needs in order to foster, facilitate, promote, and support continual improvement. These components include demonstrating leadership; initiating and encouraging growth in self and others; and engaging and supporting the development of future leaders. The skills and dispositions in this domain foster and facilitate continual improvement, promote professional learning and growth, and support school personnel.

Instructional leadership incorporates all of the must do's to provide the pressure and support teachers need to meet the requirements imposed through mandates, the district, the school, stakeholders, and other influences to elevate every student to his or her potential. These components include: demonstrates effective use of assessments; implements and supports data informed practices; provides an effective instructional program; and demonstrates purposeful planning. The skills and dispositions in this domain include championing and supporting curriculum development; advocating for instruction that supports the needs of all learners; analyzing assessments; and infusing technology to enhance learning.

Advocacy addresses the areas required of teacher leaders that sometimes prove to be the most difficult or awkward to voice. These components include: practices and refines resourcefulness; demonstrates understanding of educational policy; and supports local initiatives. The skills and dispositions in this domain demonstrate the balance teacher leaders must exhibit between administration and their teacher peers. While the teacher leader must adhere to personnel requirements and uphold rules and regulations, he or she must also model teacher voice for the advancement of resources, influence educational policy, collaborate and build relationships with both internal and external stakeholders, and create and support organizational change.

LEVELS OF PERFORMANCE

Experienced and effective school leaders hone their leadership skills and expertise over time through ongoing professional learning, reflective practice, constructive feedback, and effective supervision. It is imperative that the school leader strives for a high level of expertise within the arena of their complex work. Experience is not the same as expertise. Amount of time on the job does not automatically equate to improvement of leadership ability.

Within *The Framework for Effective Teacher Leadership* rubric, the identifiers of *levels of performance* are consistent throughout all domains. These ratings (Ineffective, Initiating, Developing, and Effective) identify the levels of performance of the teacher leader at that specific point in time. This is significant as it reflects the variability of performance, patterns of behavior, and assists in identifying areas of strengths as well as challenges. Most importantly, these levels of performance should be used as a tool for professional growth, as well as a platform for professional conversation and critical, specific feedback.

Ineffective: A leader performing at the Ineffective level does not yet demonstrate evidence of basic concepts and skills of the component. An Ineffective level can stem from a multitude of reasons including but not limited to:

- little to no understanding
- lack of prerequisite knowledge

- level of error or lack of correction of error
- lack of awareness, responsiveness, or experience
- placement in a position without necessary experience or training

Professional conversation and the development of specific professional learning goal(s) would be expected to occur and be implemented in order for the teacher leader to provide evidence of positive growth in the future. Professional conversation is also imperative to explore the core reason/s for an Ineffective rating. It is the responsibility of the evaluator or supervisor to guide the plan for improvement with the leader. Specific timelines and evidence of growth within the plan are essential.

Initiating: A leader performing at the Initiating level appears to have an understanding of the elements of the competent teacher leader, but demonstrates inconsistent implementation and application of the skills or knowledge. The Initiating level reflects the novice teacher leader who is experiencing some of the leadership experiences for the first time. It is commonly due to lack of experience that the teacher leader may identify with the Initiating level. The evaluator/supervisor of a teacher leader at the Initiating level is encouraged to implement a coaching or mentoring model to achieve positive results of professional growth. Working with the Initiating teacher leader in a supportive, yet focused, environment will provide the foundation for improved performance and improved leadership skills and dispositions.

Developing: The leader performing at the Developing level has a solid understanding of the elements of the competent teacher leader and demonstrates the ability to articulate and execute the appropriate leadership skills and/or interactions consistently with a high level of success. This level of competency is noted by others in the organization. The teacher leader is proficient, and has the capacity and skills to change course and seamlessly move to an alternate implementation plan if necessary.

Teacher leaders at the Developing level work to continually improve their practice, and members of their professional community seek them out to serve as coaches and mentors. The evaluator/supervisor of a Developing teacher leader is encouraged to be supportive of the leadership efforts and provide an appropriate platform for continued growth and success.

Effective: The teacher leader performing at the Effective level is a master of the craft. The Effective teacher leader consistently performs at the highest level with high levels of success. Educators at this level of teacher leadership are qualitatively and quantitatively different than those of their colleagues. The Effective teacher leader is a contributor to the school, community, and professional community.

Achieving an Effective level of performance does not imply a permanent rating. It is more realistic to move in and out of this distinguished area as the leadership role shifts and grows. It is also possible to not achieve the rating of Effective in all elements at the same time. The evaluator/supervisor of an Effective teacher leader is encouraged to be a champion of the leader's efforts and accomplishments.

THE NEED FOR *THE FRAMEWORK FOR EFFECTIVE TEACHER LEADERSHIP*

Identifying Targets

In working with students and districts, the authors have found a lack of understanding regarding the capacity of teacher leaders. The roles and responsibilities of teacher leaders are dependent on their district's recognition and utilization of teacher leaders. In addition, teacher leaders are often serving in capacities such as multiclassroom leaders, hybrid teacher-leaders, grade-level chairs, mentors, coaches, instructional specialists and coaches, data coaches, curriculum or assessment specialists, professional learning facilitators, PLC facilitators, master teachers, lead teachers, department chairs, directors, or deans yet they neither fit into an evaluative tool, nor are they provided with specific expectations from which they can develop professional goals. Therefore, the foundational question is "How is one to grow his or her professional skill sets if there is a moving target, or worse yet, no target at all?"

In addition, the literature review conducted identified teacher leadership initiatives dating back over thirty years; however, the literature could have very well been written today. Though an era has passed and initiatives such as Common Core State Standards, Race to the Top, and teacher accountability have had an impact, the effective use of teacher leaders continues to be presented and questioned in the same way it has been in the past.

Therefore, it is imperative to create and share a tool that frames the roles and responsibilities of teacher leaders, and encourages growth and development in these leadership roles. This tool must recognize the difference between being a teacher, an administrator, or other leadership label, and focus on the teacher leader as a bridge between classroom teachers and building administrators.

Teacher leaders must be recognized as the group of educators they are—those who have made the conscious decision to lead from the classroom. To place a teacher leader solely within a teacher's evaluation, or solely within an administrator's evaluation, does not recognize this group of individuals, their unique skills, contributions or very essence of their existence. Organizations have identified a separate set of standards and competencies, and some states have recognized teacher leaders with a separate certification, endorsement, or license so it is irresponsible to place them within a growth model or evaluation tool that does not recognize them as independent of other groups.

Commonality

While each school exhibits a culture of its own, there is a need for commonality with regard to direction and influence as reflected in the following:

1. A need for school district and school leaders to demonstrate proficiency in teacher- and administrator-evaluation processes that reflect inter-rater reliability.
2. A need for teacher leaders to share a common language and knowledge of effective models for personal and professional growth, alignment with national and state standards, and most importantly, an increase in student performance.
3. Importance for district and school leaders to have an understanding of the inter-relatedness of supervision, evaluation, and professional learning and growth.
4. Common language for professional dialogue.

It is only through commonality in these areas that we can fully understand teacher leadership in education and related organizations. It is commonality in language that fosters open professional dialogue about what defines teacher leadership, what effective teacher leadership looks like or doesn't look like, and how it is evaluated. Advocating for this foundational commonality provides the basis for professional discussions, discusses the challenges, and creates solutions while looking through the same lens of effective teacher leadership.

Self-Assessment and Reflection

The key to growth is self-assessment and reflection. We must be honest with ourselves in order to maximize our learning opportunities. Clear descriptions of expectations set the stage for personal reflection. If we are open and honest with ourselves, it is inevitable that when we read through thorough descriptions we ascertain where we are within the continuum. As seasoned practitioners we have the metacognition of knowing where we are, and a vision of where we want to be. Every person has areas in which to grow and continue in self-improvement. If we are not effective, then *The Framework* provides a clear understanding of where we ought to envision ourselves and how we set clear goals for self-improvement.

There is another area that we must openly and honestly reflect upon, and that is our relationship with others. This goes beyond our daily relationships with stakeholders; that is, personnel, students, board members, parents, community members, and so forth. We must look at ourselves as we are perceived, not as we think we project ourselves. This may call for some critical introspection and feedback for us to fully understand. It calls for us to collect data on ourselves (surveys, professional discussions, a talk with one's mentor, etc.), process, and reflect upon the feedback.

Some behaviors may be easily changed once we are aware of how we are performing or how we are perceived. However, other areas may be very difficult or even unchangeable due to our personalities. In this case, we need to carefully examine how observable behaviors impact how one functions within the organization, what can be done to strengthen relationships, or how we demonstrate commitment to the goals of the organization.

Explore Opportunities

To reform thinking that teacher leadership is merely the next step to increase one's teaching income or stature as a mentor, we must outline opportunities for teachers to see how teacher leadership can impact students and schools. This includes assistance with acquisition of new skills, the advancement of one's career, participation in decision making, development of a climate that encourages continuous learning and improvement, promotion of voice, identification of channels of leadership to those who don't wish to become principals or superintendents, participation in research, and advocating through policy, procedure, and practice.

Advocate for Teacher Leadership

The sections above demonstrate that teacher leadership has its place in the field of education. Through budget cuts, restructuring, school closures, administrative decisions, initiatives, and mandates, the teacher leader is often the one to rally—and move—the troops forward. Teacher leaders cover a variety of roles and responsibilities. Dependent on the district or school, there are variances in models, rank, title, determination specific to administration or teacher, salary, and/or stipends, benefits, and so on. While teacher leaders are essential to a school, they are often taken for granted. Therefore, the tool can serve as a resource to advocate for teacher leaders.

FOCUS ON THE PRACTITIONER

Regardless of one's role or responsibilities with the school, the ultimate goal is to increase student learning. The former *ISLLC* (2008) leadership standards, now replaced by PSEL (National Policy Board for Educational Administration 2015, 3), captured this:

> Today, educational leadership is a collaborative effort distributed among a number of professionals in schools and districts. District leaders hold positions such as superintendents, curriculum supervisors, talent management specialists, assessment directors, principal supervisors and professional learning providers. Their titles may vary, but they are all charged with the same fundamental challenge: Transform public schools to increase student learning and achievement.

To demonstrate the commonality with teacher leadership, the goal to increase student learning is also found in the Teacher Leader Model Standards (2011) in domains I and IV:

> The teacher leader understands the principles of adult learning and knows how to develop a collaborative culture of collective responsibility in the school. The teacher leader uses this knowledge to promote an environment of collegiality, trust, and respect that focuses on continuous improvement in instruction and student learning. (p. 14)

> The teacher leader demonstrates a deep understanding of the teaching and learning processes and uses this knowledge to advance the professional skills of colleagues by being a continuous learner and modeling reflective practice based on student results. The teacher leader works collaboratively with colleagues to ensure instructional practices are aligned to a shared vision, mission, and goals. (p. 17)

This was reflected in the P-20 Illinois Teacher Leadership Effectiveness Committee in 2011 (Teacher Leadership Report 2016, 3), which identified six core competencies including facilitating improvements in instruction and student learning, and accessing and using research to improve practice and student achievement. The instructional aspect of teaching is also captured in the Danielson Framework for Teaching (2013) in domain 3: engaging students in learning, and using assessment in instruction. This further exemplifies that teacher leaders are, indeed, a critical conduit and often the catalyst for transformation to actually take place.

The Framework for Effective Teacher Leadership can be used in several ways to support this collaborative effort such as evaluation, supervision, mentoring, coaching, preparation of new leadership, a guide for professional learning for current leaders, a roadmap for novice or aspiring teacher leaders, identification of targets for school improvement, and communication with the larger community. Beyond the school setting, *The Framework for Effective Teacher Leadership* can inform licensure or endorsement requirements and guide the preparation of aspiring educational leaders whether teacher leaders or future administrators. Each of these uses calls for accountability and continued growth.

Evaluation: Though this function of *The Framework for Effective Teacher Leadership* is important, the authors believe evaluation is part of a cyclical process that includes goal setting, supervision, reflection, coaching, evaluation, professional discussion, and specific feedback. *The Framework for Effective Teacher Leadership* can be used for evaluative purposes, both in formative and summative nature.

Formative Assessment: The Framework for Effective Teacher Leadership provides structured, categorized knowledge, skills, dispositions, and practices. The leader has knowledge of expectations, with clear indicators. The rubrics provide specific vocabulary that defines the level of functioning. The leader must be a reflective practitioner, and honestly and accurately place him or her within the rubric. This allows the leader to use the tool to set goals and increase level of performance through a focused practice in targeted areas.

Summative Assessment: When used as a summative tool, ongoing communication with the evaluator and evidence of each indicator creates a comprehensive picture of one's leadership. As with any summative tool, it is important to obtain data from multiple data points; therefore, the ongoing communication and evidence provides the teacher leader the opportunity to demonstrate leadership capabilities and successes across time. It is highly encouraged that *The Framework for Effective Teacher Leadership* not be used for evaluation purposes in and of itself, but as part of a process which includes coaching and ongoing professional learning and growth.

As part of the ongoing cycle, a leader should actively engage in self-evaluation, reflection, and goal-setting followed by formal evaluation, specific feedback, and goal-setting reflective of the feedback from the formal evaluation and goals of the organization. *The Framework for Effective Teacher Leadership* provides clear, articulate expectations, through which a district leader can evaluate teacher leaders accordingly.

Supervision and evaluation can be challenging for superintendents or any district leader charged with evaluating and supervising teacher leaders. Creating an ongoing and effective supervision and evaluation process is necessary to the climate and health of the district and the schools. *The Framework for Effective Teacher Leadership* can be used as a tool to guide this process. It helps to set the stage for ongoing mentoring, coaching, and formal evaluations required by boards of education and also required for employment decisions.

Mentoring: This step is often skipped at the teacher leadership level. It's assumed that once a leadership position is obtained at the district or building level, one will be self-sufficient, figure things out, and resourceful enough to obtain the assistance needed to succeed. While we see the benefits of mentoring teachers and increasing retention if teachers are properly oriented, trained, and supported, the isolation of building or district teacher leaders creates a barrier few districts have sought to overcome.

Knowing and understanding expectations provides a foundation on which those new to leadership positions can build. Providing *The Framework for Effective Teacher Leadership* takes the guesswork out of what is supposed to be done and provides a level of understanding to the process. Just as teachers are provided time to acclimate and grow in their positions, so must leaders, and so must teacher leaders.

Coaching: Teacher leaders need a professional network that they can trust will be confidential. Teacher leaders have questions, but may believe they can't go to their superior or they will be viewed as incompetent or less than capable. Some teacher leaders find themselves geographically or systemically separated from other teacher leaders, so they find it difficult to talk to their peers about challenges or problems they are facing.

Coaching is productive as it provides a safe place to openly discuss challenges or miscues within a nonevaluative and nonjudgmental setting, and offers the opportunity to celebrate successes. It provides a safe place to exchange ideas and the opportunity to receive feedback to provide direction and growth. *The Framework for Effective Teacher Leadership* provides specific knowledge, skills, dispositions, and practices from which the teacher leader or the coach can identify areas of focus for practice or improvement.

Preparation of New Teacher Leadership: Regardless of the size of the district or school, there are opportunities to build leaders from within. It is inevitable that there are faculty or staff members who display leadership skills or dispositions. There needs to be dialogue with them about their aspirations. Some may aspire to move into an administrative position in the future, while others may aspire to lead from the classroom while continuing to teach.

The Framework for Effective Teacher Leadership provides a comprehensive guide to inform current leaders in recruiting and cultivating prospective teacher leaders. The development of *The Framework* reflects understanding of the new teacher leader through the use of the Initiating level of performance. This performance indicator specifically reflects skills and dispositions of a new teacher leader just beginning one's journey. As a progressive continuum, the expectation is that this is a beginning point, and the teacher leader will grow through experience and continued professional development and training.

Professional Learning and Growth: When developing professional learning opportunities for staff, considerations must be made regarding current initiatives, needs of the school, interests of the staff, and training or professional learning needs of the staff—in other words, what does that individual need to be successful in his or her current setting and role? Teacher leaders need the same considerations. *The Framework for Effective Teacher Leadership* is a guide for professional learning for current teacher leaders in that it lays out the knowledge, skills, dispositions, and practices of effective teacher leaders. As reflective practitioners, this guide is used to target areas of need or interest of further development.

Roadmap: Novice or aspiring teacher leaders often do not have a level of understanding of what effective teacher leadership looks like, nor do they know the questions to ask. It's difficult to formulate meaningful questions on a topic you don't really understand. Therefore, *The Framework for Effective Teacher Leadership* provides a roadmap for novice or aspiring teacher leaders in that it lays out what effective teacher leadership looks like, as well as providing specific knowledge, skills, dispositions, and practices from which the novice can choose to focus to practice and obtain experience.

School Improvement: Education has evolved into a field where its leaders are accountable for providing evidence of effective district or school leadership as indicated by students' readiness for college, careers, and life. Public perception of preparation of such skills for students is filtered from the leader, through the teachers, and into the students; therefore, student success is directly linked to effective leadership.

School improvement has evolved from policies and procedures, to accountability for the academic success and well-being of every student. Therefore, if improvements are needed in the school, there is call for leadership to be responsive. Teacher leaders are, indeed, a critical conduit and often the catalyst for transformation to actually take place. *The Framework for Effective Teacher Leadership* provides specific knowledge, skills, dispositions, and practices that can directly be linked to mission, vision, values, and goals of the district or school.

Communication: *The Framework for Effective Teacher Leadership* provides the benefit of common language. Whether speaking to an administrator, board member, community member, or parent the same terminology is used. Educational jargon has been removed to reveal practical, real-life knowledge, skills, dispositions, and practices that can be understood by, and communicated to, the community at large.

Licensure/Endorsement and Preparation: *The Framework for Effective Teacher Leadership* provides clear, articulate expectations of teacher leaders. Candidates in preparatory programs for teacher leadership or seeking licensure, certification, or endorsement are shaped by the use of *The Framework for Effective Teacher Leadership*. Through familiarity, active interaction with, and reflection on *The Framework for Effective Teacher Leadership*, candidates practice skills and behaviors directly aligned with standards in which they are required to demonstrate proficiency to obtain licensure (certification or endorsement).

National Board for Professional Teaching Standards (NBPTS): The Framework for Effective Teacher Leadership aligns with and supports the five propositions identified by NBPTS. These five propositions are:

- Teachers are committed to students and their learning.
- Teachers know the subjects they teach and how to teach those subjects to students.
- Teachers are responsible for managing and monitoring student learning.
- Teachers think systematically about their practice and learn from their experience.
- Teachers are members of learning communities.

The National Board for Professional Teaching Standards (NBPTS) has a continuum that moves the teacher from preservice to novice, to professional, to board certified, to teacher leader. This continuum demonstrates the recognition of teacher leadership as an extension beyond the ability to demonstrate knowledge and skills to positively impact student learning; benefit from ongoing professional learning and growth; or being shaped by licensure, evaluation, and professional development provided to and for the teacher. The teacher leader, or educational leader as referenced by NBPTS, provides a platform to grow professionally and become leaders at multiple levels: school, district, state, and profession. In addition, the teacher leader is called on to develop the next generation of accomplished practitioners; facilitate system improvement; and support colleagues along the continuum.

SUMMARY

The purpose of this chapter is to examine observable behaviors through which teacher leaders can be supervised, evaluated, coached, mentored, provided opportunity to practice, and anchored in a model that promotes professional learning and growth. This chapter explains the development and format of *The Framework for Effective Teacher Leadership*. The four domains of *The Framework for Teacher Leadership* include: domain 1—*critical competencies*; domain 2—*professional growth of self and others*; domain 3—*instructional leadership*; and domain 4—*advocacy. The Framework for Effective*

Teacher Leadership has two main parts: *The Framework* and the rubrics that align with *The Framework.*

The rubrics reflect each component within the four domains and are broken down to capture the essential information of the elements within that component. The rubric reflects the levels of performance for each of the elements. Through use of this tool, elements aligned with standards and competencies provide specific guidance helpful in self-reflection of personal strengths and areas in need of improvement to enhance performance and increase effectiveness of teacher leaders.

SELF-ASSESSMENT AND REFLECTION

In a study conducted by Leithwood and Riehl (2004, pp. 6–7), three core practices are identified for effective leaders: setting direction, developing people, and developing the organization. Also in the study, one of three conclusions specific to the impact on student learning is who educational leaders should pay close attention to—teachers! Specifically, their pedagogical content knowledge and professional communities both inside and outside the school (Leithwood and Riehl 2004, p. 11).

Reflect on your educational environment. Who comes to mind when you think of leaders among teachers? What observable behaviors do they exhibit that bring them to the forefront when you think of teacher leaders? Are they currently in formal or informal teacher leader roles? Do they take on additional responsibilities without being asked, or accept them unconditionally when asked?

Now consider yourself. How do you view yourself within the framework of teacher leadership? How might others view you?

REFERENCES

Center for Teaching Quality, National Board for Professional Teaching Standards, and the National Education Association. (2014). *The teacher leadership competencies.* Carrboro, NC: Center for Teaching Quality.

Danielson, C. (2007). *Enhancing professional practice: A framework for teaching.* Alexandria, VA: Association for Supervision and Curriculum Development.

DuFour, R., DuFour, R., Eaker, R., and Many, T. (2010). *Learning by doing.* Bloomington, IN: Solution Tree Press.

Leithwood, K., Louis, K., Anderson, S., and Wahlstrom, K. (2004). *How leadership influences student learning.* St. Paul, MN: Center for Applied Research and Educational Improvement, University of Minnesota.

Lieberman, A. (1992). Teacher leadership: What are we learning? In C. Livingston, (Ed.), *Teachers as leaders: Evolving roles*. NEA School Restructuring Series. Washington, DC: National Education Association.

National Policy Board for Educational Administration. (2018). National Educational Leadership Preparation 2018. Reston, VA: Author.

———. (2015). Professional Standards for Educational Leaders 2015. Reston, VA: Author.

National Board for Professional Teaching Standards (NBPTS). (2017). *What teachers should know and be able to do*. Retrieved from http://www.nbpts.org/standards-five-core-propositions/

OpportunityCulture.org. (2014). *Teacher-led professional learning to reach every student with excellent teachers: Defining teacher-leader roles*. Chapel Hill, NC: Public Impact.

Strike, K., Sims, P., Mann, S., and Wilhite, R. (2016). *Transforming professional practice: A framework for effective leadership*. Lanham, MD: Rowman and Littlefield.

Teacher Leadership Exploratory Consortium. (2008, 2011). *Teacher leader model standards*. Washington, DC: National Education Association (NEA).

Wheatley, M. (2006). *Leadership and the new science: Discovering order in a chaotic world*. San Francisco: Barrett-Kohle.

Chapter Five

The Framework for Effective Teacher Leadership: Domains 2 and 3

OBJECTIVES

Throughout this chapter you will:

1. Understand the expectations and introspection of domains 2 and 3 of *The Framework* (NELP 1, 2, 3, 4, 5, 6, 7; PSEL 1, 2, 3, 4, 5, 6, 7, 8, 9, 10; TLMS 1, 2, 3, 4, 5, 6, 7).
2. Explore *The Framework for Effective Teacher Leadership* domain 2 (NELP 1, 2, 4, 6; PSEL 1, 2, 3, 4, 5, 6, 7, 9, 10; TLMS 1, 3, 4, 6).
3. Examine rubrics for domain 2 (NELP 1, 2, 4, 6; PSEL 1, 2, 3, 4, 5, 6, 7, 9, 10; TLMS 1, 3, 4, 6).
4. Explore *The Framework for Effective Teacher Leadership* domain 3 (NELP 1, 3, 4; PSEL 1, 2, 3, 4, 5, 6, 7, 10; TLMS 1, 2, 3, 4, 5, 6, 7).
5. Examine rubrics for domain 3 (NELP 1, 3, 4; PSEL 1, 2, 3, 4, 5, 6, 7, 10; TLMS 1, 2, 3, 4, 5, 6, 7).
6. Examine applications of *The Framework* (NELP 1, 2, 3, 4, 5 ,6, 7; PSEL 1, 2, 3, 4, 5, 6, 7, 8, 9, 10; TLMS 1, 2, 3, 4, 5, 6, 7; NBPTS 4, 5).

EXPECTATIONS AND INTROSPECTION —DOMAINS 2 AND 3

This chapter examines the collective observable behaviors of effective teacher leaders through the lens of rubrics and narrative descriptors derived from *The Framework for Effective Teacher Leadership*. Taking into consideration that teacher leadership is a bridge between classroom teachers and building administration, the indicators within each rubric reflect representation of PSEL (2015) and NELP (2017) leadership standards, and the Model Teacher Leader Standards (2011). The National Board for Professional Teaching Standards five core propositions are also represented.

The Framework for Effective Teacher Leadership reflects knowledge, skills, dispositions, and practices required of those serving as teacher leaders. Roles that reflect teacher leadership specific to domain 2—*professional growth of self and others*, and domain 3—*instructional leadership* include but are not limited to department chair; dean; grade or department team lead; building leadership team; mentor; coach; school or district improvement member; curriculum team; action researcher; professional development coordinator; peer review; professional portfolio reviewer; assessment, literacy, or technology coach; data analyzer; book study facilitator; or certification/licensure/endorsement assistance.

Internal decisions within the district determine the terminology used to describe a role as well as role(s) that may be held by teacher leaders and the coordinating responsibilities. Therefore, how the framework is used as well as application of the framework to develop a professional learning plan will vary.

The Framework for Effective Teacher Leadership identifies observable knowledge, skills, and practices recognized and sought in effective teacher leaders. These observable behaviors are framed in a way that provides continuity and offers a platform for inter-rater reliability. Therefore, *The Framework* provides a common resource reflecting common language based on standards of practice.

Dispositions are embedded within *The Framework* rather than separate. Dispositions of Effective teacher leaders include but are not limited to being energetic risk-takers whose integrity, high efficacy, and content knowledge give them credibility with their colleagues; desire to work with adults; a belief that systems-level change will positively impact student learning; natural curiosity makes them lifelong learners; value different ideas and approaches to move work forward; deep sense of courage; unwavering perseverance; open to constructive criticism; reflective; and resilient (CSTP 2009, p. 3).

THE FRAMEWORK FOR EFFECTIVE TEACHER LEADERSHIP: DOMAIN 2—PROFESSIONAL GROWTH OF SELF AND OTHERS

In addition to the identification of indicators are narrative descriptions of each indicator. Descriptors are important because they provide thoughtful and reflective explanations that enhance the value of the activity; make actions more thoughtful, purposeful and rewarding; ensure high quality; and establish the foundation for deeper and more productive professional conversations.

In an effort to maximize professional learning and growth, a narrative description of each component is provided. This description clarifies the rationale and reflects the level of skill that demonstrates effective teacher leadership. The narrative descriptors are not meant to be comprehensive in nature, but provide specific examples of behaviors exhibited in effective teacher leaders.

Rationale and Explanation

In domain 2, the focus is the *professional growth of self and others*. This domain includes three essential components:

2a: Demonstrates leadership
2b: Initiates and encourages growth of self and others
2c: Engages and supports the development of future leaders

These components also include essential elements of each of these practices, as well as levels of performance for each of the elements contained within each of the components. When viewed holistically, this domain can serve as a guide for both the teacher leader and the evaluator/supervisor in order to ascertain current levels of performance and to set forth goals for future professional growth.

2a: Demonstrates Leadership

The first component within domain 2 is *demonstrates leadership*. Teacher leaders work to continuously hone leadership skills from the classroom, which necessitates a unique skill set that is different from those skills that are required of the building leader. Effective teacher leaders facilitate the development of a culture that is supportive of innovative thinking and risk-taking efforts.

This culture is essential in order for student-centered, personalized teaching practices to flourish within classrooms. Within this type of culture, educators are willing to try new teaching methods to meet all student needs. They may also experiment with cutting-edge technological practices, new methods of assessment, or classroom-management innovations.

In addition, Effective teacher leaders seek out opportunities in which they are able to model flexibility and the establishment of safe, nonjudgmental relationships. Risk-taking and innovative thinking both within and outside of the classroom cannot take place without these types of relationships as the firm basis of support. Furthermore, Effective teacher leaders are able to precisely discern and communicate their own needs and the needs of their colleagues in order to advance their own professional practices, as well as the professional practices of fellow educators.

For example, a teacher leader might determine through formative assessment practices that students lack a common language for specific reading decoding skills. He or she might further ascertain through collaborative team meetings that this is a concern in classrooms throughout the school building. The teacher leader might take steps to address this common need through planned professional development for multiple grade levels that addresses this core need for a common language when working with students on decoding strategies. The impact of the teacher leader is seen and felt well beyond his or her classroom when addressing the issue.

Finally, within the component *demonstrates leadership*, Effective teacher leaders have a firm handle on their own and others' capacities for distributed leadership and the advancement of collective wisdom. The Effective teacher leader, when confronted with the need for building-wide professional development on decoding strategies as presented above, might activate emergent teacher leaders in facilitating professional development and collaborating to promote the change initiative.

Essentially, the Effective teacher leader has clear insight as to where the current knowledge base is and how to grow each stakeholder, pushing forward with consistent support and motivation to assure enhanced practices in every classroom throughout the school building.

2b: Initiates and Encourages Growth of Self and Others

The second component within domain 2 is *initiates and encourages growth of self and others*. This component is an essential piece of continuous improvement efforts within all school environments. In order for widespread beneficial change to take place, teacher leaders must seek out appropriate leadership roles and opportunities extending beyond one's classroom.

Operating within the silo of one's own classroom is no longer a viable option in today's connected and ever-changing learning environments. It is essential that teachers model for both students and colleagues the importance of reaching beyond the classroom learning environment in order to have a broader impact on the growth of all stakeholders.

Likewise, teacher leaders take a leading role in technological innovation and transformation for communication, advocacy, management, networking, learning, and teaching. Technological advancements occur at a rapid pace, and the skilled teacher leader stays abreast of these changes and seamlessly incorporates new strategies into research-based teaching practices in order to both enrich the student learning environment and to assure that students are adept at utilizing varying forms of technological innovation within their everyday lives.

As Effective teacher leaders facilitate the growth of themselves and others, they also make connections to education, economic, and social trends and policy in planning and facilitating professional learning experiences. These practices prepare students for the ever-changing world that they will one day contribute to through their future employment and engagement with society.

Finally, Effective teacher leaders actively engage in, practice, and encourage inquiry, research, and sharing information with all educational stakeholders. Teacher leaders take an active role in bridging the gap between the educational research community and schools/classrooms. For example, if a particular subgroup of students is not showing growth in math, Effective teacher leaders examine research-based practices to determine what proven methods of instruction are most likely to have a positive impact within the particular subgroup.

This research takes place prior to determining the best course of action within the learning environment and is conducted in conjunction with colleagues in order to encourage the practices of inquiry and collaboration in addressing future classroom needs.

2c: Engages and Supports the Development of Future Leaders

The final component within domain 2 is *engages and supports the development of future leaders*. This component assures that the cycle of mentorship and support that teachers provide to their colleagues carries on as new educators are inducted into the profession and as seasoned teacher leaders impart priceless wisdom and guidance that comes from years of experience in the field.

Likewise, educators who are new to the profession can provide leadership in innovative practices that comes from their more recent engagement in educator preparation programs. Thus, teacher leaders are nurtured and developed from the moment they step into the classroom and are able to contribute to the growth of one another in two-way learning opportunities that are beneficial to both experienced and newly minted teacher leaders.

As Effective teacher leaders facilitate and support the growth of their colleagues, they engage these individuals based on intimate knowledge of their colleagues' strengths, personality, styles, practices, and beliefs. This type of differentiation is key to maximizing the growth of adult learners, just as it is key to the development of students within the classroom.

Furthermore, Effective teacher leaders make meaningful and relevant connections to their colleagues' work with intentionality based on personal goals and interests. They can articulate ways in which they advance leadership capacity through varied methods that build competence, confidence, and capacity with their fellow educators.

In order to assure that professional growth takes place within the educational environment, Effective teacher leaders pose thought-provoking questions, engage in difficult conversations, and immerse themselves in professional dialogue that uncovers and challenges prior assumptions and beliefs. For example, if the teacher leader discerns that a specific teaching practice is no longer meeting student needs, yet is still being used, he or she will capitalize on the strong and trusting relationships built with his or her colleagues to critically examine the effectiveness of the teaching practice.

This questioning and examination of the potentially ineffective teaching practice is conducted in such a way that fellow educators feel respected and engaged in the change process. As a result, the teacher leader builds the efficacy of others through self-management, self-monitoring, and self-modification.

THE FRAMEWORK FOR EFFECTIVE TEACHER LEADERSHIP: DOMAIN 3—INSTRUCTIONAL LEADERSHIP

For each of the domains within *The Framework for Effective Teacher Leadership*, narrative descriptors for each indicator are provided in order to set forth a clear picture of educational practices that clarify and define each aspect of teacher leadership within *The Framework* for the reader.

Each description is structured in such a way that it provides a narrative description, sets forth the rationale for the necessity of the educational practice, and reflects the level of skill that is indicative of Effective teacher leadership. Each narrative description is not intended to be comprehensive, but rather to set forth specific examples of effective practices for teacher leaders.

Rationale and Explanation

In domain 3, the focus is the *instructional leadership* of the teacher leader. This domain includes four essential components:

3a: Demonstrates effective use of assessments
3b: Implements and supports data-informed practices
3c: Provides an effective instructional program
3d: Demonstrates purposeful planning

These components are also broken down into essential elements of each of these practices in order to provide clarity for each component.

Table 5.1. Rubrics for Domain 2—Professional Growth of Self and Others

2a: Demonstrates leadership	*Level of Performance*			
Element	*Ineffective*	*Initiating*	*Developing*	*Effective*
Supports innovative thinking and risk-taking efforts	Does not support innovative thinking and risk-taking efforts	Limited support of innovative thinking and risk-taking efforts	Actively encourages support of innovative thinking and risk-taking efforts	Builds a culture supportive of innovative thinking and risk-taking efforts
Models flexibility and establishes safe, nonjudgmental relationships	Does not show evidence of flexibility and/or establishment of safe, nonjudgmental relationships	Attempts to but may not always be able to model flexibility and establish safe, nonjudgmental relationships	Efficiently models flexibility and establishes safe, nonjudgmental relationships	Prepares opportunities to model flexibility and establish safe, nonjudgmental relationships
Identifies and communicates needs of self and others to advance shared goals and job-embedded professional learning	Fails to identify and/or communicate needs of self and others to advance shared goals and job-embedded professional learning	Lacks clarity in identification and communication of needs of self and others to advance shared goals and job-embedded professional learning	Efficiently identifies and communicates needs of self and others to advance shared goals and job-embedded professional learning	Precisely identifies and communicates needs of self and others to advance shared goals and job-embedded professional learning
Develops the capacity for distributed leadership and encourages collective wisdom	Fails to build capacity and/or fails to encourage collective wisdom	Attempts to develop with limited success the capacity for distributed leadership and encourages collective wisdom	Actively encourages the capacity for distributed leadership and encourages collective wisdom	Self-assesses the capacity for distributed leadership and encourages collective wisdom

(continued)

Table 5.1. *(continued)*

2b. Initiates and encourages growth in self and others	*Level of Performance*			
Element	*Ineffective*	*Initiating*	*Developing*	*Effective*
Seeks appropriate leadership roles and opportunities extending beyond one's classroom	Fails to seek appropriate leadership roles and opportunities extending beyond one's classroom	Attempts but may not always seek appropriate leadership roles and opportunities extending beyond one's classroom	Models and upholds appropriate leadership roles and opportunities extending beyond one's classroom	Establishes and reinforces appropriate leadership roles and opportunities extending beyond one's classroom
Leads technological innovation and transformation for communication, advocacy, management, networking, learning, and teaching	Fails to lead technological innovation and transformation for communication, advocacy, management, networking, learning, and teaching	May not clearly lead technological innovation and transformation for communication, advocacy, management, networking, learning, and teaching	Clearly and accurately leads technological innovation and transformation for communication, advocacy, management, networking, learning, and teaching	Provides varied options to lead technological innovation and transformation for communication, advocacy, management, networking, learning, and teaching
Uses education, economic, and social trends and policy in planning and facilitating professional learning	Fails to use education, economic, and social trends and policy in planning and facilitating professional learning	Articulates use of education, economic, and social trends and policy in planning and facilitating professional learning	Supports through a variety of strategies the use of education, economic, and social trends and policy in planning and facilitating professional learning	Makes meaningful and relevant connections between education, economic, and social trends and policy in planning and facilitating professional learning

Practices and encourages inquiry, research, and sharing information	Fails to practice and encourage inquiry, research, and sharing information	Attempts to practice and encourage inquiry, research, and sharing information with limited success	Models and upholds practices and encourages inquiry, research, and sharing information	Actively engages in practices and encourages inquiry, research, and sharing information

2c. Engages and supports the development of future leaders	*Level of Performance*			
Element	*Ineffective*	*Initiating*	*Developing*	*Effective*
Empowers and engages individuals for success based on a knowledge of strengths, personality, style, practices, and beliefs	Fails to empower and engage individuals for success based on a knowledge of strengths, personality, style, practices, and beliefs	Inconsistently empowers and engages individuals for success based on a knowledge of strengths, personality, style, practices, and beliefs	Demonstrates an understanding of how to empower and engage individuals for success based on a knowledge of strengths, personality, style, practices, and beliefs	Differentiates to empower and engage individuals for success based on a knowledge of strengths, personality, style, practices, and beliefs
Aligns individual's work with intentionality based on goals and interests	Fails to align individual's work with intentionality based on goals and interests	Inconsistently aligns individual's work with intentionality based on goals and interests	Shows evidence of ability to align individual's work with intentionality based on goals and interests	Makes meaningful and relevant connections to individual's work with intentionality based on goals and interests

(continued)

Table 5.1. *(continued)*

2c. Engages and supports the development of future leaders	*Level of Performance*			
Element	*Ineffective*	*Initiating*	*Developing*	*Effective*
Demonstrates interpersonal effectiveness through articulation of ways to support others to build competence, confidence, and capacity	Fails to demonstrate interpersonal effectiveness through articulation of ways to support others to build competence, confidence, and capacity	Inconsistently demonstrates interpersonal effectiveness through articulation of ways to support others to build competence, confidence, and capacity	Shows evidence of interpersonal effectiveness through articulation of ways to support others to build competence, confidence, and capacity	Advances leadership capacity and interpersonal effectiveness through articulation of ways to support others to build competence, confidence, and capacity
Transforms others through thought-provoking questioning, difficult conversations, and engaging in professional dialogue that uncovers assumptions and beliefs	Fails to transform others through thought-provoking questioning, difficult conversations, and engaging in professional dialogue that uncovers assumptions and beliefs	Attempts to transform others through thought-provoking questioning, difficult conversations, and engaging in professional dialogue that uncovers assumptions and beliefs	Actively engages in transformation of others through thought-provoking questioning, difficult conversations, and engaging in professional dialogue that uncovers assumptions and beliefs	Advances transformation of others through thought-provoking questioning, difficult conversations, and engaging in professional dialogue that uncovers assumptions and beliefs
Builds efficacy through self-management, self-monitoring, and self-modification	Fails to build efficacy through self-management, self-monitoring, and self-modification	Attempts to build efficacy through self-management, self-monitoring, and self-modification	Practices building efficacy through self-management, self-monitoring, and self-modification	Appropriately adapts to build efficacy through self-management, self-monitoring, and self-modification

In addition, levels of performance for each of the elements are clarified and set forth within *The Framework for Effective Teacher Leadership*. Domain 3 of *The Framework* can be utilized in order to analyze areas of strength and areas to target for growth when examining the instructional leadership practices of teacher leaders in all stages of development.

3a: Demonstrates Effective Use of Assessments

The first component within domain 3 is *demonstrates effective use of assessments*. Effective teacher leaders use multiple procedures to collect and report evidence of student learning. This practice is critical in order to assure that all students within every classroom have demonstrated mastery of specific learning outcomes throughout the course of the school year.

Teacher leaders also extend this analysis of student learning to the students themselves, engaging learners in monitoring their own growth. This can be done using multiple strategies, including the use of goal-setting, the use of self-assessments, and the use of student data graphs/charts to track individual progress throughout the school year.

Effective teacher leaders also facilitate compliance measures and lead the preparation of local, state, and federal reporting. They understand and communicate with others about the importance of obtaining, analyzing, and responding to multiple measures of student learning to improve instructional practices.

Furthermore, they continuously increase the capacity of their colleagues to effectively use multiple assessment tools in order to meet individualized student learner needs. This appropriate and high-impact use of assessment data enriches each student's learning, each teacher's instructional practices, and each classroom's effectiveness in achieving positive learning outcomes.

3b: Implements and Supports Data-Informed Practices

The second component within domain 3 is *implements and supports data-informed practices*. This component works in tandem with the first component within domain 3, *demonstrates effective use of assessments*, to assure that the usage of all data is aimed at continuous instructional improvement. The Effective teacher leader not only initiates the design, implementation, evaluation, and analysis of student data, but also leads the reflective analysis, the collaborative interpretation and communication of results, and the application of findings to improve teaching and learning.

Essentially, the teacher leader collaboratively facilitates all aspects of data collection and analysis, as well as the implementation of goals and instructional improvements that result from the careful review of and reflection on multiple sources of data. These leaders develop a collaborative culture in which educators design individual and rigorous collaborative learning opportunities that encourage positive social interaction, active engagement in learning, and self-motivation.

These strategies are based upon the Effective teacher leader's extensive knowledge base of research-based best practices that are carefully researched and matched to specific student learning needs unique to each learner and/or each classroom.

3c: Provides an Effective Instructional Program

The third component within domain 3 is *provides an effective instructional program.* This component is critical to the overall success of students, classrooms, and schools that are served by the Effective teacher leader. These leaders initiate the collaboration with administration to provide teachers time, support, and training necessary to create and administer assessments; collect, analyze, reflect on, and report data; and set goals.

This partnership between building leaders and teacher leaders is a key component of an Effective leadership structure that meets the needs of all stakeholders. In addition, the effective teacher leader accurately anticipates the needs of each learner and proactively implements strategies to improve student learning. This practice is also coordinated in conjunction with fellow educators, as well as the building leader, in order to impact both the teacher leader's classroom as well as the overall school environment.

Within the collaborative professional environment, the Effective teacher leader also creates, advocates for, and consistently implements instruction that meets the needs of all learners. For example, if students within the classroom environment have learning needs that fall above or below grade-level expectations, the Effective teacher leader seamlessly differentiates instructional plans to incorporate individualized learning opportunities that promote the engagement and growth of every learner within the classroom.

Furthermore, the Effective teacher leader uses multiple strategies to harness the skills, expertise, and knowledge of colleagues to address curricular expectations and student learning needs. Ideally, these practices take place within a well-planned and effectively implemented collaborative meeting structure during which educators routinely plan for instructional improvement to meet student learning needs.

3d: Demonstrates Purposeful Planning

The fourth and final component within domain 3 is *demonstrates purposeful planning.* As noted above, this purposeful planning should be viewed as a valuable and essential professional practice, and, as such, should be a top priority for the building leader, the teacher leader, and all educators throughout the school environment.

The Effective teacher leader initiates this planning to promote instruction that supports every student meeting rigorous learning goals and outcomes and transference to practice. Furthermore, the Effective teacher leader also consistently infuses relevant technology to enrich curriculum and instruction, matching strategies to meet individual student learning needs.

In addition, within their purposeful planning practices, Effective teacher leaders initiate the continual use of developmental, learning, and motivational theories to learning (cognitive, linguistic, social, emotional, and physical). These leaders insist that they and their colleagues understand and utilize what is known about student learning to ensure that individual needs are met and student growth is sustained at an optimal level.

Effective teacher leaders also focus their plans on these individualized student learning needs specifically relating to classroom management, content, instruction, and assessment. Finally, these plans are set forth with the use of research-based best practices that support and advance instruction. The Effective teacher leader may also engage in such research to further contribute to the field of education.

APPLICATIONS OF *THE FRAMEWORK*

Coaching, Mentoring, Supervision, and *The Framework*

As explained by Darling-Hammond (2013), there is a distinction between teacher quality and teaching quality. Teacher quality is the personal characteristics that an educator brings to the teaching profession, including qualities such as a strong content knowledge of the subject area to be taught, knowledge of how to teach the content to others, and an understanding of how to support diverse learners in their academic growth (Darling-Hammond 2013).

Teaching quality, on the other hand, is distinct from the above teacher qualities because teaching quality is strongly impacted by the context of instruction, including factors aside from what the teacher knows and can do (Darling-Hammond 2013). If an educator with strong teacher qualities does not have all of the supports needed (environment, curriculum, teaching conditions) to provide high-quality instruction, teaching quality and teacher effectiveness is negatively impacted (Darling-Hammond 2013).

Thus, coaching and mentoring are essential aspects that are integral to the growth and development of teacher leaders to assure that teaching quality meets the developing and effective levels of *The Framework for Effective Teacher Leadership*. As teachers grow toward the developing and effective levels of

Table 5.2. Rubrics—Domain 3 Instructional Leadership

3a: Demonstrates effective use of assessments	*Level of Performance*			
Element	*Ineffective*	*Initiating*	*Developing*	*Effective*
Collects and reports evidence of student learning	Does not collect and/or does not report evidence of student learning	Makes an attempt to collect and report evidence of student learning but is not completely successful	Successfully collects and reports evidence of student learning	Uses multiple procedures to collect and report evidence of student learning
Understands and uses multiple methods of assessment to engage learners in own growth, monitor learner progress, and guide teachers and learners in decision making	Fails to understand and/or use assessments to monitor learner progress or guide decision making	Attempts to use assessments to monitor learner progress and/or guide decision making, but may rely on one method or is minimally successful	Understands and uses multiple methods of assessment to monitor learner progress and guide decision making.	Understands and uses multiple methods of assessment to monitor learner progress and guide decision making, as well as to effectively engage learners in monitoring their own growth
Assists with compliance and preparation of local, state, and federal reporting	Does not assist with compliance and preparation of local, state, and federal reporting	Inconsistently assists with compliance and preparation of local, state, and federal reporting	Actively assists with compliance and preparation of local, state, and federal reporting	Facilitates compliance measures and leads the preparation of local, state, and federal reporting
Increases the capacity of colleagues to effectively use multiple assessment tools based on purpose, use, and reporting of assessment	Fails to enhance colleagues' capacity to effectively use multiple assessment tools based on purpose, use, and reporting of assessment	Attempts to increase the capacity of colleagues to effectively use multiple assessment tools based on purpose, use, and reporting of assessment, but may experience minimal success or may cause confusion	Increases the capacity of colleagues to effectively use multiple assessment tools based on purpose, use, and reporting of assessment	Continuously increases the capacity of colleagues to effectively use multiple assessment tools based on purpose, use, and reporting of assessment to meet the full range of student learner needs

3b: Implements and supports data informed practices	*Level of Performance*			
Element	*Ineffective*	*Initiating*	*Developing*	*Effective*
Assists with design, implementation, evaluation, and analysis of student data	Does not assist with design, implementation, evaluation, and analysis of student data	Makes an attempt to assist with design, implementation, evaluation, and analysis of student data but is not completely successful	Consistently and successfully assists with design, implementation, evaluation, and analysis of student data	Initiates the design, implementation, evaluation, and analysis of student data
Assists in accessing data, reflective analysis, collaborative interpretation of results, application of findings to improve teaching and learning, and communication of results	Fails to assist in accessing data, reflective analysis, collaborative interpretation of results, application of findings to improve teaching and learning, or communication of results	Demonstrates some familiarity with accessing data, reflective analysis, collaborative interpretation of results, application of findings to improve teaching and learning, and communication of results	Continuously assists in accessing data, reflective analysis, collaborative interpretation of results, application of findings to improve teaching and learning, and communication of results	Facilitates the accessing of data, and leads reflective analysis, collaborative interpretation of results, application of findings to improve teaching and learning, and communication of results
Collects and uses data to identify goals and promote learning	Does not collect or use data to identify goals and promote learning	Inconsistently collects and uses data to identify goals and promote learning	Consistently collects and uses data to identify goals and promote learning	Initiates the collection and use of data to identify goals and promote learning

(continued)

Table 5.2. *(continued)*

3b: Implements and supports data informed practices	*Level of Performance*			
Element	*Ineffective*	*Initiating*	*Developing*	*Effective*
Designs individual and rigorous collaborative learning that encourages positive social interaction, active engagement in learning, and self-motivation	Fails to design individual and rigorous collaborative learning that encourages positive social interaction, active engagement in learning, and self-motivation	Attempts to design individual and rigorous collaborative learning that encourages positive social interaction, active engagement in learning, and self-motivation with minimal success	Appropriately designs individual and rigorous collaborative learning that encourages positive social interaction, active engagement in learning, and self-motivation	Develops a collaborative culture in which educators design individual and rigorous collaborative learning that encourages positive social interaction, active engagement in learning, and self-motivation

3c: Provides an effective instructional program	*Level of Performance*			
Element	*Ineffective*	*Initiating*	*Developing*	*Effective*
Collaborates with administration to provide teachers time, support, and training necessary to create and administer assessments; collect, analyze, reflect on, and report data; and set goals	Does not collaborate with administration to provide teachers time, support, and training necessary to create and administer assessments; collect, analyze, reflect on, and report data; and set goals	Collaborates on a limited basis with administration to provide teachers time, support, and training necessary to create and administer assessments; collect, analyze, reflect on, and report data; and set goals	Actively collaborates with administration to provide teachers time, support, and training necessary to create and administer assessments; collect, analyze, reflect on, and report data; and set goals	Initiates collaboration with administration to provide teachers time, support, and training necessary to create and administer assessments; collect, analyze, reflect on, and report data; and set goals

Adapts practice to meet the needs of each learner and improve student learning	Fails to adapt practice to meet the needs of each learner and improve student learning	Inconsistently adapts practice to meet the needs of each learner and improve student learning	Consistently adapts practice to meet the needs of each learner and improve student learning	Accurately anticipates the needs of each learner and proactively implements strategies to improve student learning
Advocates for instruction that supports the needs of all learners	Does not advocate for instruction that supports the needs of all learners	Inconsistently advocates for instruction that supports the needs of all learners	Consistently advocates for instruction that supports the needs of all learners	Creates, implements, and consistently advocates for instruction that supports the needs of all learners
Harnesses the skills, expertise, and knowledge of colleagues to address curricular expectations and student-learning needs	Misses opportunities to harness the skills, expertise, and knowledge of colleagues to address curricular expectations and student-learning needs	Partially harnesses the skills, expertise, and knowledge of colleagues to address curricular expectations and student-learning needs	Continuously harnesses the skills, expertise, and knowledge of colleagues to address curricular expectations and student-learning needs	Uses multiple strategies to harness the skills, expertise, and knowledge of colleagues to address curricular expectations and student-learning needs.

3d: Demonstrates purposeful planning	*Level of Performance*			
Element	*Ineffective*	*Initiating*	*Developing*	*Effective*
Plans or collaborates to promote instruction that supports every student meeting rigorous learning goals/outcomes and transference to practice	Fails to plan or collaborate to promote instruction that supports every student meeting rigorous learning goals/outcomes and transference to practice	Inconsistently plans or collaborates to promote instruction that supports every student meeting rigorous learning goals/outcomes and transference to practice	Consistently plans or collaborates to promote instruction that supports every student meeting rigorous learning goals/outcomes and transference to practice	Initiates planning or collaboration to promote instruction that supports every student meeting rigorous learning goals/outcomes and transference to practice

(continued)

Table 5.2. *(continued)*

3d:Demonstrates purposeful planning	*Level of Performance*			
Element	*Ineffective*	*Initiating*	*Developing*	*Effective*
Infuses relevant technology to enrich curriculum and instruction	Rarely or never infuses relevant technology to enrich curriculum and instruction	Partially infuses relevant technology to enrich curriculum and instruction	Continuously infuses relevant technology to enrich curriculum and instruction	Consistently infuses relevant technology to enrich curriculum and instruction, matching strategies to meet individual student learning needs
Applies developmental, learning, and motivational theories to learning (cognitive, linguistic, social, emotional, and physical)	Does not apply developmental, learning, and motivational theories to learning (cognitive, linguistic, social, emotional, and physical)	Explains but does not consistently incorporate developmental, learning, and motivational theories to learning (cognitive, linguistic, social, emotional, and physical)	Consistently incorporates developmental, learning, and motivational theories to learning (cognitive, linguistic, social, emotional, and physical)	Initiates continual use of developmental, learning, and motivational theories to learning (cognitive, linguistic, social, emotional, and physical)
Focuses on student learning specific to classroom management, content, instruction, and assessment	Does not plan with a focus on student learning specific to classroom management, content, instruction, and assessment	Partially focuses on student learning specific to classroom management, content, instruction, and assessment	Thoroughly plans with a focus on student learning specific to classroom management, content, instruction, and assessment	Thoroughly plans with a focus on individualized student learning specific to classroom management, content, instruction, and assessment
Accesses, uses, and/or engages in research to support and advance instruction	Does not access, use, or engage in research to support and advance instruction	Occasionally accesses, uses, and/or engages in research to support and advance instruction	Continuously accesses, uses, and/or engages in research to support and advance instruction	Initiates the access, use of, and/or engagement in research to support and advance instruction

performance within domains 2 and 3 of *The Framework*, they may exhibit some leadership practices within the Initiating level as detailed within the rubric.

Typically, novice teachers who have an understanding of these essential leadership practices and who attempt to demonstrate leadership in some situations or who inconsistently implement these leadership practices fall within this level. Coaching and mentoring, along with a plan for professional growth and support will help the novice teacher to develop and gain confidence within these domains.

Likewise, teachers new to the profession may demonstrate some of the behaviors that fall in the Ineffective level, often due to a lack of skills or a lack of knowledge. It is imperative that the evaluator/supervisor, as well as other teacher leaders, guide and coach the beginning teacher in such a way that leadership skills start to emerge and are practiced on a regular basis.

Experienced teacher leaders who consistently demonstrate the leadership components, as set forth within the rubric, have a solid understanding of each of the elements that comprise domain 2—*professional growth of self and others* and domain 3—*instructional leadership*. They consistently implement these leadership practices and have built the capacity of themselves and their colleagues through continual expansion of their own and others' skill sets.

They are proficient educators who mentor, coach, and support their colleagues. They adjust the course of action as needed to effectively meet student and adult learner needs. These teacher leaders typically exhibit practices that fall within the Developing to Effective levels of performance within the rubric. Effective teacher leaders are always further developing and refining their professional practices, and this is why they don't typically attain a permanent rating of Effective in all areas of performance.

The Effective level of performance connotes that the teacher leader is a master of the craft in a particular area, and their practice within that area sets them apart from their colleagues. Within educational communities, this level of performance is frequently visited by accomplished teacher leaders, but it is not a place where they permanently reside. Rather, they continually revisit the Developing level of performance, while pushing forward to the Effective teacher leader level of performance in specific areas and at specific times as needed within the learning environment (Marzano and Toth 2013).

Effective Supervision, Constructive Evaluation, and *The Framework*

The Framework for Effective Teacher Leadership has been developed to serve multiple purposes for both teacher leaders and the administrators who supervise, evaluate, and support their work. By defining the specific, yet widely variant, roles and responsibilities that teacher leaders fulfill, a common language is developed from which supervision and evaluation can take place.

Furthermore, by recognizing and specifying the growth that occurs throughout the career span of teacher leaders, both the teacher leader and his or her supervisors are able to concisely ascertain the levels at which the teacher leader is currently operating and set reasonable yet rigorous goals for professional growth. In order for administrators to effectively supervise and evaluate teacher leaders within each domain of *The Framework for Effective Teacher Leadership*, they must have a firm grasp of the components, elements, and levels of performance that comprise each domain (Partee 2012).

Domain 2—*professional growth of self and others*, and domain 3—*instructional leadership*, set forth the following essential components of both of these domain areas. When nurtured within the aspiring teacher leader, the components result in professional growth both within the teacher leader and within those educators who are mentored, coached, and supported by the teacher leader.

Effective supervision and evaluation of professional growth can further enhance the development of the teacher leader. It should be noted that the extent to which the teacher leader experiences this growth as part of the evaluative process is largely dependent upon the appropriate implementation of an overall evaluation system utilized by the administrator. *The Framework for Effective Teacher Leadership* can and should be used as a tool to collaboratively examine current teacher practice and set forth goals and action steps to further professional growth as a part of an overall comprehensive system of support and evaluation (Little, 2009).

Also key to this process is a strong and trusting relationship between the evaluator and the teacher leader. The process of self-reflection requires that the teacher leader makes himself or herself vulnerable by critically and honestly identifying and naming areas of strength and areas of weakness. This level of trust cannot be achieved in a school environment that lacks support and/or mutual respect. Thus, there is a significant responsibility placed upon the evaluator to assure that the evaluative environment is ideal in order to facilitate productive conversations that will result in improved professional practice.

In addition, in order to reflect on his or her work within domains 2 and 3, the teacher leader must be given ample opportunity to lead from the classroom. This leadership includes but is not limited to any of the following: facilitating grade-level, department-level, and/or school-wide meetings; leading change initiatives; supporting/mentoring colleagues; analyzing school data and planning for improvement; and providing outreach to stakeholders to engage the community at large.

This level of involvement requires a culture of shared leadership that is created and nurtured by the building leader. The level of success that the teacher leader is able to achieve is at least partially dependent upon the collaborative atmosphere developed and sustained by the building leader (Marshall 2009). Finally, it is important to recognize that time is an essential element as it relates to domains 2 and 3 and as it relates to the evaluative process.

Both of these domains require that teacher leaders reflect thoroughly on their personal growth, as well as how they have worked to inspire professional growth in others. Reflection, while critical to improvement, can often be overlooked in the busy school environment where time is at a premium. Thus, it is essential that both the teacher leader and the evaluator devote time to the critical process of reflection on a consistent and continual basis. Ideally, reflection should be prioritized on a daily basis, as each task is completed and/or as each collaborative interaction takes place.

SUMMARY

This chapter explores domains 2 and 3 of *The Framework for Effective Teacher Leadership*. Domain 2 focuses on *professional growth of self and others*, while domain 3 sets forth the critical aspects of *instructional leadership* as it relates to effective teacher leaders. A narrative description is provided for each component within these two domains of the rubric, as well as a rationale for the necessity of each of the leadership practices. Finally, the level of skill that is necessary for effective teacher leadership is set forth, and coaching, mentoring, and the supervision of teacher leaders within each of these domains is examined.

SELF-ASSESSMENT AND REFLECTION

You have now read and examined domain 2—*professional growth of self and others* and domain 3—*instructional leadership* of *The Framework for Effective Teacher Leadership*. In your experience as an aspiring teacher leader, give examples of specific teacher-leadership practices that you have been engaged in that fall within each of these two domains. Within which of the domains, components, and/or elements were you more effective and which areas do you need to focus on for future growth? Explain steps you can take to further develop in areas where you need to continue to grow as a teacher leader, opportunities you can seek to gain additional experience, and possible resources—including personnel—you will seek.

REFERENCES

CSTP. (2009). *Teacher leadership skills framework.* Olympia, WA: Center for Strengthening the Teaching Profession.

Darling-Hammond, L. (2013). *Getting teacher evaluation right: What really matters for effectiveness and improvement.* New York: Teacher College Press.

Little, O. (2009). Teacher evaluation systems: The window for opportunity and reform. Retrieved from https://www.ohea.org/Document/Get/16584

Marshall, K. (2009). *Rethinking teacher supervision and evaluation.* San Francisco, California: Jossey-Bass.

Marzano, R. J. and Toth, M. D. (2013). Teacher evaluation that makes a difference: A new model for teacher growth and student achievement. Alexandria, VA: ASCD.

Partee, G. L. (2012). Using multiple evaluation measures to improve teacher effectiveness. Retrieved from http://www.americanprogress.org/issues/education/report/2012/12/18/48368/using-multiple-evaluation-measures-to-improve-teacher-effectiveness/

Chapter Six

The Framework for Effective Teacher Leadership: Domains 1 and 4

OBJECTIVES

Throughout this chapter you will:

1. Understand the expectations and introspection of domains 1 and 4 of *The Framework* (NELP 1, 2, 3, 4, 5 ,6, 7; PSEL 1, 2, 3, 4, 5, 6, 7, 8, 9, 10; TLMS 1, 2, 3, 4, 5, 6, 7).
2. Explore *The Framework for Effective Teacher Leadership* domain 1 (NELP 1, 2, 4, 6; PSEL 1, 2, 3, 4, 5, 6, 7, 9, 10; TLMS 1, 3, 4, 6).
3. Examine rubrics for domain 1 (NELP 1, 2, 4, 6; PSEL 1, 2, 3, 4, 5, 6, 7, 9, 10; TLMS 1, 3, 4, 6).
4. Explore *The Framework for Effective Teacher Leadership* domain 4 (NELP 1, 3, 4; PSEL 1, 2, 3, 4, 5, 6, 7, 10; TLMS 1, 2, 3, 4, 5, 6, 7).
5. Examine rubrics for domain 4 (NELP 1, 3, 4; PSEL 1, 2, 3, 4, 5, 6, 7, 10; TLMS 1, 2, 3, 4, 5, 6, 7).
6. Examine applications of *The Framework* (NELP 1, 2, 3, 4, 5 ,6, 7; PSEL 1, 2, 3, 4, 5, 6, 7, 8, 9, 10; TLMS 1, 2, 3, 4, 5, 6, 7; NBPTS 4, 5).

EXPECTATIONS AND INTROSPECTION —DOMAINS 1 AND 4

This chapter examines the collective observable behaviors of effective teacher leaders through the lens of rubrics and narrative descriptors derived from *The Framework for Effective Teacher Leadership*. Taking into consideration that teacher leadership is a bridge between classroom teachers and building administration, the indicators within each rubric reflect representation of PSEL (2015) and NELP (2017) leadership standards, and the Model Teacher Leader Standards (2011). The National Board for Professional Teaching Standards five core propositions are also represented.

The Framework for Effective Teacher Leadership reflects knowledge, skills, dispositions, and practices required of those serving as teacher leaders. Roles that reflect teacher leadership specific to domain 1—*critical competencies* and domain 4—*advocacy* include but are not limited to committee member; advocate; accreditation specialist; policy influence; building liaison; task-force member; creation of partnerships (organizations, businesses, universities, etc.); presenting at a conference; leading initiatives; serving on parent-teacher organizations; developing procedures to meet stakeholders' needs; or teaching on special assignment.

Internal decisions within the district determine the terminology used to describe a role as well as role(s) that may be held by teacher leaders and the coordinating responsibilities. Therefore, how *The Framework* is used as well as application of *The Framework* to develop a professional learning plan will vary.

The Framework for Effective Teacher Leadership identifies observable knowledge, skills, and practices recognized and sought in effective teacher leaders. These observable behaviors are framed in a way that provides continuity and offers a platform for inter-rater reliability. Therefore, the framework provides a common resource reflecting common language based on standards of practice.

Dispositions are embedded within the framework rather than separate. Dispositions of effective teacher leaders include but are not limited to the ability to collaborate with others, enlist colleagues to support their vision, build consensus among diverse groups of educators, and inform others of the importance of what they propose and the feasibility of their plan for improvement; possesses instructional skills that are well respected by their colleagues; continuously perseveres; does not allow setbacks to derail an important initiative; understands evidence and information to yield gains in student learning; is optimistic, enthusiastic, confident, decisive, open-minded and respectful of others' opinions, as well as flexible and willing to try a different approach; is an active listener and facilitator; keeps people on track; and decides a course of action and monitors the progress (Danielson 2007).

What motivates the elementary classroom teacher to expand her role to impact teaching and learning in her grade, her school, her district or beyond? What knowledge, skills, dispositions and practices does the middle-school Spanish teacher need to influence board-level policy decisions? What must high-school teachers first understand, believe, and share about the community's values and district mission to lead a critical change?

How can an elementary teacher stay in the classroom, but create a career path that impacts teaching and learning in a powerful and rewarding way? Through exploration of *The Framework for Effective Teacher Leadership* and corresponding rubrics, questions such as these are contemplated through the lens of critical competencies in domain 1 as foundational skills for teacher leaders and the skills in domain 4 that are illustrative of advocacy. In addition to the identification of indicators, there are narrative descriptions of each indicator.

Descriptors are important because they provide thoughtful and reflective explanations that enhance the value of *The Framework*; make actions such as coaching and mentoring more thoughtful, purposeful, and rewarding; ensure high-quality evaluation; and establish the foundation for deeper and more productive professional conversations. In an effort to maximize professional learning and growth, a narrative description of each component and element is provided.

This description clarifies the rationale. The tables that follow then reflect the level of skill that demonstrates ineffective, initiating, developing or effective teacher leadership. The narrative descriptors are not meant to be comprehensive in nature, but provide specific examples of behaviors exhibited in effective teacher leaders.

THE FRAMEWORK FOR EFFECTIVE TEACHER LEADERSHIP: DOMAIN 1—*CRITICAL COMPETENCIES*

Rationale and Explanation

Domain 1 is the conduit through which teachers move from focus solely on teaching to begin a conversation about understanding and developing the skills of teacher leadership, skills that are the foundation for the many roles of teacher leaders. In domain 1 there are four components and fifteen elements.

1a: Values and Draws Upon the Culture and Community One Serves

The first component, *values and draws upon the culture and community one serves*, raises consciousness about the context in which teacher leaders serve and the importance of appreciating and understanding that context in all leadership conversations and form decisions that the teacher leader undertakes. Context, culture, and the community matter.

This component provides an important lens that the teacher leader must use to filter and form decisions that best serve the students in any community. Those decisions include and revolve around the four elements of component 1:

- Advances the mission, vision, and goals of the school
- Advocates for a mindful culture that reflects equity, fairness, and diversity
- Initiates cultural responsiveness, and
- Maintains professionalism in all interactions.

As teacher leaders work, they must not only know the mission, vision, and goals of the school/district/ initiative, but they must see the integral link between the ideals that are established to guide the work in a community and the culture that is being served. The concept of service is important as it refers to the idea of putting the welfare of others before one's own.

Thus, the community being served is key as there are many good decisions that can be made by leaders, but if the decision does not serve the values, beliefs, and traditions of the community, it will not be a good fit for the community and will not contribute or add value to the lives and well-being of the students in the community.

For example, an Effective-level teacher leader moves a district forward while keeping the history of an event in mind. During a heated debate about mathematics adoption in a district, Effective teacher leaders share their past experience and successfully guide the committee to a recommendation that reflects the best fit for the community and student population it serves.

These teacher leaders use recommendations of multiple stakeholders, historical knowledge of the community and its culture, and teacher-led proposals and consider the mission, vision, and goals of the district. Functioning at the Effective level, these teacher leaders have a positive, powerful impact on student learning.

Similarly, teacher leaders must advocate for a mindful culture that reflects equity, fairness, and diversity. The Effective teacher leader is conscious of and mindful of both his internal and external thoughts and actions about equity, fairness, and diversity. Equity does not suggest that when decisions are made everyone gets the same, but rather that the needs of each determine the level of support provided (Tomlinson 2014).

So, varying degrees of support are provided in an equitable but fair manner. Fairness then refers to the possibility that each student can meet expectations because he has the level of support that attempts to counter the level of need in a just way (Council of Chief State School Officers 2015, p. 10). An effective teacher leader is not only mindful of equity, fairness, and diversity, but the Effective teacher leader fosters the same mindfulness in others to create an environment and culture where the knowledge and values of equity, fairness, and diversity are shared by all.

For example, teachers develop a student-driven research project with students matched with mentors in the field chosen to research. As part of the program evaluation, a Developing teacher leader recognizes students of color had not enrolled nor had students with less natural ability. The program is successfully modified to reflect recruitment of students with proportional representation and accommodations for special education students.

Initiates cultural responsiveness is an element that goes well beyond the teacher leader respecting and being sensitive to attitudes and beliefs about culturally and linguistically diverse students and community members, their languages, cultures, and life experiences. Effective teacher leaders must acknowledge, develop, assess, and advocate for policies and procedures, as well as materials, strategies, and activities that promote cultural identities and mutual respect among and between students, parents, staff, and community members (Khalifa et al. 2016).

For example, in many schools, teachers are expanding their work well beyond classroom walls and campus boundaries. Culturally responsive Developing teacher leaders take their lessons into the communities where families feel comfortable and safe, such as at the YMCA, the church, the community center, or the park. They teach more than academics during these outreach sessions, instead focusing on matters such as navigating the school system, identifying resources for tutoring and counseling, preparing for the ACT and SAT, developing parent networks, managing the college application process, and more.

Finally, the Effective teacher leader *maintains professionalism in all interactions*. Because the Effective teacher leader upholds the mission, vision, values, and goals of the school and district, is mindful and promotes both mindfulness and cultural identities and mutual respect, it follows that the Effective teacher also maintains professionalism in all interactions.

For teachers who are transitioning from effective teachers to Effective teacher leaders, that means going beyond reflecting on teaching, maintaining accurate records, communicating with families, contributing to the school and district, growing and developing professionally and showing professionalism (Grady, Helbling, and Lubeck, 2008). It means demonstrating and modeling professionalism and appropriate teacher conduct, as well as encouraging professionalism among all stakeholders. Even in times of disagreement, professionals must check their attitude, communication, and demeanor.

For example, while some teachers may agree with a committee recommendation, others will disagree. The Effective teacher leader works to preserve the collaborative caring school culture, do what is best for the students, and reach a compromise. The Effective teacher leader facilitates dialogue focused on alternatives that best fit the needs of the school, students, and staff, and reconvenes the committee to discuss scenarios that promote compromise. The Effective teacher leader provides expertise and communicates and acts in a professional manner to support the committee work rather than individual work.

1b: Engages All Stakeholders

The second component, *engages all stakeholders*, reminds the Effective teacher leader to bring all segments of a population that might be affected by a decision into all decisions, decisions regarding issues, problems, and decisions about policies and procedures, curriculum, and instruction and operations.

The elements break the component down and stress that an Effective teacher leader:

- Examines problems and issues from multiple perspectives and connects ideas,
- Builds community through a concerted collaborative effort to reach out to disenfranchised or disengaged populations,
- Provides outreach and collaboration with families and community in response to community needs, and
- Responds to needs and accomplishments of stakeholders.

The first element, *examines problems and issues from multiple perspectives and connects ideas*, is integral to the success of the Effective teacher leader. This element may also mark a decisive change in behavior from the effective teacher to the Effective teacher leader. While teachers must rely consistently on their individual ability to examine problems and connect their own thoughts and ideas, appending the word "leader" to "teacher" designates the essential move to a broad consideration of multiple perspectives and ideas of others.

Builds community through a concerted collaborative effort to reach out to disenfranchised or disengaged populations is wise advice for the teacher leader. This element reinforces the practice of reaching out to fringe stakeholders who for one reason or another have disassociated themselves from the school or education establishment. Learning more about those outsiders, understanding their needs and the actions that alienated them, can map a route for the Effective teacher leader to connect and then collaborate with all groups to create a stronger sense of community.

When all groups connect and there is a strong sense of community, the actions taken by leadership thrive in a supportive environment. Conversely, when some stakeholders feel like outsiders, the disconnect affects the likelihood of success on any front.

For example, paraprofessionals perform essential services but can be marginalized and relegated to menial clerical tasks. Developing teacher leaders, recognize an individual's work, contributions and value. Through active listening, they take time to understand needs and concerns; find ways to improve their own relationships, communication and instruction; and identify ways in which paraprofessionals and teacher leaders can work together to make a positive difference in the lives of their students.

Similarly, Effective teacher leaders must always take into consideration how decisions and actions address the needs of the community. Effective teacher leaders may think they know the needs of the community they serve, but it is wise to reach out and collaborate with all segments of the community so that each group feels they are heard and represented. Reaching out to the community and bringing all segments to the decision table ensures that the decisions made have been well vetted and will be implemented with fidelity.

For example, the Effective teacher leader recognizes the effectiveness of current communication practices used with English Language Learners. Rather than continuing the status quo, the Effective teacher leader seeks to improve communication with all groups of stakeholders, and seeks input from various sources. The information is not only collected, but analyzed. A plan is developed and changes are implemented to increase effective communication.

Finally, the Effective teacher leader recognizes the contributions of all stakeholders, considers the strength of each idea, and looks for connections across a variety of ideas. Using someone's idea, even if modified slightly, acknowledges the stakeholder. Thus, using multiple ideas and connecting them invests everyone in the solution and strengthens the solutions derived. Any acknowledgement is a celebration, but the teacher leader must also commend the group for its hard work through public acknowledgement and sometimes even private celebration.

People work harder when they know they are being heard, their ideas are valued, and their work is appreciated. In a study by Amabile and Kramer (2011), clear goals, autonomy, and nourishing colleagues can uplift workers. This included encouragement, respect, and collegiality by fellow workers and supervisors. The four broad categories they found to significantly impact workers were: (1) respect; (2) encouragement; (3) emotional support; and (4) affiliation (Andrews 2011, 62).

For example, a Developing teacher leader demonstrates active listening with students' growing concern about excessive homework. The teacher leader listens while students volunteer a possible resolution. The teacher leader brings both the concern and the recommendation to the staff. Staff support the change. The principal brings this information to the district leadership meeting where it is also supported. This change becomes common practice and builds morale.

1c: Attains Student Success in the Classroom

The third component is *attains student success in the classroom*. While student success is most frequently identified with standardized achievement tests, teacher leaders may make their colleagues and supervisors aware of alternate tools the teacher leader uses for assessing student success, such as performance assessments and measures of confidence, growth mindset, and interest.

This component is best illustrated by examining its three elements: applies and models best practices for student learning; utilizes knowledge of content areas, curriculum, cross disciplinary skills, and pedagogy; and draws on knowledge of the cultural and community context.

The first element is *applies and models best practices for student learning.* Best practices refers to practices that have been found, through research, to provide or supply skills to learners. Effective teacher leaders not only rely on and use best practices in their own classroom, but they encourage their colleagues to use best practices by demonstrating how to access, implement, and assess the use of best practices in the classroom.

The second element is *utilizes knowledge of content area, curriculum, cross-disciplinary skills and pedagogy*. The Effective teacher leader not only knows the content, but understands how curriculum is structured and what pedagogy best fits the content and curriculum selected.

For example, an Effective elementary teacher leader attends a series of professional-development workshops. Convinced by the evidence he has seen in the model project schools, the research results he read, and the practices he has learned in simulations, the teacher leader believes that the model reflects best practice and meets the needs of the students with whom he works. He shares his new knowledge and information with staff, the principal, and district-level decision makers.

The changes yield positive results in student learning, and the teacher leader serves as a conduit to advance the use of these practices in classrooms across the district, observes other classrooms to ensure fidelity to the program, and coaches teachers to maximize student learning.

In addition to content, curriculum, and pedagogy, the teacher leader also *draws on knowledge of the learner, and cultural and community contexts*—the third element in this domain. Effective teacher leaders draw on a number of components to design instruction that best meets the needs of their students. In classrooms that are increasingly diverse, Effective teacher leaders get to know their students and use this knowledge to enhance instruction and entice learning.

Effectiveness includes not only applying the elements in one's own classroom but also being able to share the ideas in such a way that others are able to effectively implement the concepts and ideas in their own classrooms. For example, through change of practice in her classroom, an early childhood teacher better meets students' needs. These changes lead to parent support, and the opportunity to network and advocate for early childhood education.

As a result, she is invited to provide testimony to support early childhood education at a state legislative appropriation hearing focused on funding. This Effective teacher leader not only changes practice to better meet the needs of the students and parents she serves, but has a voice that affects students across the state.

1d: Models Effective Coaching Skills

The fourth component, *models effective coaching skills*, identifies skills that are used to prompt or cue an individual when they are engaged in teaching, learning or leading. It is exemplified by four elements: establishes an environment of trust, confidentiality, and respect; engages in direct and appropriate communication; establishes a presence to build relationships across professional communities; and provides active listening and alternatives, as well as specific feedback, relevant application, details, and reflection.

To be an effective coach, it is imperative to create *an environment of trust, confidentiality, and respect.* Effective teacher leaders understand that professional growth is personal. It requires being honest with oneself about areas of strength and need. That kind of intimate work can only be accomplished in a safe environment where respect for the teacher as learner is central. The Effective teacher leader structures the environment so that it is clear that the coach has only one motive—professional growth.

For example, an Ineffective teacher leader is unable to advance a teacher's instruction in the classroom. The development and refinement of coaching skills are foundational to the teacher leader. Building relationships, aligning teachers' behaviors with the teaching standards, and understanding the teacher's teaching style are vital. Although the teacher leader may coach and provide some feedback, factors such as superficial, minimal, meaningless, or untimely feedback hamper growth, and lack of trust destroys it. If a relationship is not developed, the teacher is reluctant and coaching can never advance.

Direct and appropriate communication in element two draws attention to the important role one's style of interaction plays in being an effective coach. Direct communication is articulate, honest, and forthright. Effective teacher leaders say what they mean—there's no pretense. Effective teachers listen carefully, act as a sounding board, and provide carefully thought out feedback that is specific and meaningful.

This is one of the more challenging aspects of teacher leadership. Criticism, no matter how constructive or well-meaning, is understandably likely to be met with defensiveness. Teacher leaders must be exceptionally specific in providing kind and forthright guidance based on careful observation.

For example, a Developing teacher leader may focus on just one or two areas in each coaching session with her teachers. Examples and nonexamples of the critical practice the teacher was working on may be shared in an effort to better see opportunities to enhance instruction. Targeted and specific feedback result in successful student learning and productive, long-term, trusting relationships.

Establishes a presence is perhaps one of the more challenging concepts to define as it refers to one's manner, behavior, or demeanor. Effective teacher leaders behave in a way that disarms the meek or disgruntled and others and helps them feel comfortable, valued, and trusted. Presence sets the tone for a productive working relationship where conversation, goal-setting, and healthy risk-taking flourish.

Presence is not just established in coaching sessions or staff meetings. It is established across the school by *walking the talk* of a growth mindset, of being both a learner and a teacher, and by truly seeking first to understand before being understood. Presence goes hand in hand with trust and teachers will trust those teacher leaders who advocate for a greater good, acknowledge their own limitations, live and breathe the school's vision and culture, and are serious about attaining goals that matter.

For example, the Effective teacher leader clearly communicates and assures that others understand the *why* of important decisions made at all levels. The Effective teacher leader questions, probes, elaborates, investigates, and explores other options with regard to how the *why* connects to the school or district's mission, vision, and goals. The Effective teacher leader demonstrates an eagerness to learn through engaging in professional learning sessions, staff meetings, and professional learning communities both advancing new ideas and nurturing those of others.

Finally, in component 4, Effective teacher leaders provide active listening, alternatives, specific and meaningful feedback, and relevant application and details. This element emphasizes the importance of reflection and meaningful feedback in the coaching scenario. The Effective teacher leader understands the importance of providing cues and setting goals with teachers or others that teacher leaders may mentor or coach.

The teacher leader makes it clear that the focus is not on where a teacher performs right now, but where that teacher is going and how he or she can best get there by listening and providing feedback that suggests helpful alternatives and clear details to strengthen and advance teacher performance.

The Effective teacher leader also recognizes the importance of each teacher's unique craft and artistry as a teacher and shines a bright light on choice and a variety of paths that lead to success in the classroom. When an Effective teacher leader's work is done, the teachers he or she works with are invested and share a sense of accomplishment.

Table 6.1. Rubrics for Domain 1—Critical Competencies

1a: Values and draws upon the culture and community one serves	*Level of Performance*			
Element	*Ineffective*	*Initiating*	*Developing*	*Effective*
Advances the mission, vision, and goals of the school	Does not work to develop or uphold the mission, vision, values, and goals of the school	Can explain the mission, vision, values, and goals of the school but does not consistently develop and uphold them	Accurately explains the mission, vision, values, and goals of the school and upholds and develops them with some degree of consistency	Creates an environment where the mission, vision, values, and goals of the school thrive
Advocates for a mindful culture that reflects equity, fairness, and diversity	Fails to establish a mindful culture where equity, fairness, and diversity are valued	Attempts to establish a mindful culture that reflects equity, fairness, and diversity by identifying the elements	Establishes some of the elements of a mindful culture that reflects equity, fairness, and diversity	Creates a mindful culture where actions reflect equity, fairness, and diversity in all endeavors
Initiates cultural responsiveness	Fails to initiate cultural responsiveness	Understands the elements of and is sometimes able to demonstrate cultural responsiveness	Explains and endorses cultural responsiveness and reinforces its use	Models and encourages cultural responsiveness in all aspects of the educational setting
Maintains professionalism in all interactions	Demonstrates a lack of professionalism in interactions	Demonstrates a knowledge of some elements of professionalism in interactions with some audiences	Demonstrates all elements of professionalism in interactions with most audiences	Models and encourages professionalism among all groups in all interactions

(continued)

Table 6.1. *(continued)*

1b: Engages all stakeholders	*Level of Performance*			
Element	*Ineffective*	*Initiating*	*Developing*	*Effective*
Builds community through a concerted collaborative effort to reach out to disenfranchised or disengaged populations	Misses or declines the opportunity to reach disenfranchised or disengaged populations and build a community	Values community and begins to use some strategies to connect with some populations on a limited basis	Collaborates and builds community with some populations regularly	Connects with all populations to build community
Provides outreach and collaboration with families and community in response to community needs	Fails to recognize community needs and collaborate with families and the community to address those needs	Reaches out to and collaborates with some families and members of the community	Understands needs within the stakeholder population and gathers with families and the community to find solutions	Models strategies for understanding and using community needs to reach out to families and members of the community to collaborate
Responds to needs and accomplishments of stakeholders	Does not see and misses opportunities to respond to the needs and accomplishments of stakeholders (colleagues, staff, parents, students)	Attempts to encourage and respond to the development of others	Promotes the development of other stakeholders	Encourages and actively seeks out and celebrates the success of all stakeholders
Examines problems and issues from multiple perspectives and connects ideas	Utilizes a narrow and self-serving lens for examining problems and issues	Gives some consideration to other perspectives in examining issues and problems	Examines problems and issues from multiple perspectives and attempts to connect ideas	Encourages all perspectives and connects ideas to arrive at good solutions for addressing all problems and issues

1c: Attains student success in the classroom	*Level of Performance*			
Element	*Ineffective*	*Initiating*	*Developing*	*Effective*
Applies and models best practices to student learning	Fails to use best practices to affect student learning	Identifies best practices for instruction and attempts to apply and model best practices for student learning	Demonstrates best practices for successful student learning	Models and applies best practices for successful student learning and shares and encourages the use of best practices with colleagues
Utilizes knowledge of content areas, curriculum, cross-disciplinary skills, and pedagogy	Fails to articulate and use knowledge of content areas, curriculum, cross-disciplinary skills, and pedagogy	Articulates and sometimes uses knowledge of content areas, curriculum, cross-disciplinary skills, and pedagogy to achieve successful student learning	Articulates and consistently applies a knowledge of content areas, curriculum, cross-disciplinary skills, and pedagogy to achieve student success	Articulates, applies, and models knowledge of content areas, curriculum, cross-disciplinary skills, and pedagogy to achieve student success beyond his classroom
Draws on knowledge of the learner's cultural and community context	Fails to understand, value, or draw on knowledge of the learner's cultural and community context	Values drawing on knowledge of the learner's cultural and community context and attempts to use this knowledge in planning instruction	Understands, appreciates, and draws on knowledge of the learner's cultural and community context in planning instruction	Creates a learning environment in which educators draw on knowledge of the learner's cultural and community context

(continued)

Table 6.1. *(continued)*

1d: Models effective coaching skills	*Level of Performance*			
Element	*Ineffective*	*Initiating*	*Developing*	*Effective*
Establishes an environment of trust, confidentiality, and respect	Fails to understand and establish an environment of trust, confidentiality, and respect	Values yet is unable to establish an environment of trust, confidentiality, and respect	Establishes an environment of trust, confidentiality, and respect	Establishes an environment of trust, confidentiality, and respect and encourages others to value and create a respectful environment
Engages in direct and appropriate communication	Fails to engage in direct and appropriate communication	Understands the tenets of direct and appropriate communication and tries it	Demonstrates direct and appropriate communication	Creates an environment where direct and appropriate communication are valued and modeled consistently
Establishes a presence to build relationships across professional communities	Fails to build relationships across professional communities	Attempts to develop relationships in some professional communities	Builds a strong working relationship in and across multiple professional communities	Helps colleagues access varied options to establish a presence to build relationships across professional communities
Provides active listening, alternatives, specific and meaningful feedback, relevant application, details, and reflection	Fails to listen and rarely provides alternatives or provides inappropriate feedback, application, and details to daily work	Listens and tries to provide appropriate feedback and share application ideas and details	Listens and provides feedback, shares applications, and can clearly articulate details	Creates an environment that embraces active listening, alternative means of instruction, specific and meaningful feedback, relevant applications, illustrious details, and opportunity for reflection

The Effective teacher leader is not necessarily trying to change the teacher's unique style of teaching, but rather helping that teacher learn and grow to evaluate and change his or her own actions and find successful student learning through focused coaching, compassionate relationships, and ample opportunities for supported practice.

For example, the Effective teacher leader provides guidance on one or two ways to improve the craft, models it as needed, and reinforces it frequently with specific, positive, and varied feedback. The Effective teacher leader utilizes multiple approaches based on the teacher, the teacher's needs, and alignment to the task, such as one-on-one conferences, side-by-side video analysis, or observation of a colleague.

The Effective teacher leader not only monitors but also recognizes progress, and lets the teacher know this progress is recognized through a handwritten note, card, or even a small token of accomplishment. The Effective teacher leader incorporates a growth mindset approach that focuses on the importance of encouraging effort, accepting stumbles, sharing ideas and stories, and contemplating possibilities. Target behaviors evolve, and the teacher sees progress and learns through this process. Continual growth is encouraged, supported, and desired.

THE FRAMEWORK FOR EFFECTIVE TEACHER LEADERSHIP: DOMAIN 4—*ADVOCACY*

Advocacy, or public support for students, policy, and procedures focuses on an Effective teacher leader's area of knowledge and skill that may or may not permeate through other components of teacher leadership. However, you can readily see how advocacy is both needed for and connected with the critical competencies listed in domain 1. Support for students and learning revolves around issues of resources, policy, and local initiatives. Thus, in domain 4 there are three components and eleven elements.

4a: Practices and Refines Resourcefulness

The first component, *practices and refines resourcefulness*, includes mobilizing community resources as well as school resources. Financial, human, and material resources are all an integral part of the Effective teacher leader's repertoire, along with relevant professional development and training. Essential, too, is a knowledge of the social service agencies that serve a community or school. But it is not enough to know of the resources; an Effective teacher leader also knows how to access those resources and make them available for others.

It is challenging for one person to know everything about the resources in a community or school, so networking and making connections with multiple people is essential. The Effective teacher leader understands that it is imperative to create a give-and-take collaborative culture where a working knowledge of resources is readily shared to meet the needs of all learners.

For example, when school districts are faced with budget cuts, the decisions are often made with little input from all the stakeholders. Art and music are often the first to go or be cut back followed by a reduction in classified staff and increased class sizes. But using the combined wisdom of several groups, a Developing teacher leader preserves the arts in a school by working with teacher, parent, and student groups to make a compelling research-based case coupled with real-life examples from schools for reducing expenditures in other areas that would preserve the art leadership (and thus the art program) and student learning.

4b: Demonstrates an Understanding of Educational Policy

While the ability to access resources to support teaching and learning is critical to advocacy for effective teacher leaders, it is important to remember that the work of education is done in a larger political, social, economic, legal, and cultural context that is quite complex. Component 2 of advocacy, then, is *demonstrating an understanding of educational policy*: How does the political, social, economic, legal, and cultural context work in a school community? What are the factors that inform and influence decisions? Are they local, state, or national? What are the opportunities to enter into the decisions about a school or educational community? Advocacy is often an aspect of education that is uncomfortable for teachers. Teachers often feel that they have little to offer. However, that need not and cannot be the case. Teacher voice matters in schools, districts, and legislatures.

Unlike board members, administrators, mayors, and legislators, teachers work directly with students and thus have a highly credible and potentially powerful voice. Effective teacher leaders develop a culture that encourages teacher voice to lead and respond to matters of education policy and procedures.

Within that culture, the teacher leader encourages listening to others and seeing multiple perspectives to build bridges with all stakeholders and strengthen both opportunity and access to the decision-making table. Effective teacher leaders model and encourage others to step up and out of the classroom to serve at school, district, state, or national levels to shape and implement education policy.

For example, an Effective teacher leader can enter a controversial situation, enlist the aid of peers, invite input of stakeholders, highlight experiences,

Table 6.2. Rubrics for Domain 4—Advocacy

4a. Practices and refines resourcefulness	*Level of Performance*			
Element	*Ineffective*	*Initiating*	*Developing*	*Effective*
Mobilizes community resources to support student achievement, solve problems, and achieve goals	Fails to mobilize community resources to support student achievement, solve problems, and achieve goals	Attempts to mobilize community resources to support student achievement, solve problems, and achieve goals	Actively mobilizes community resources to support student achievement, solve problems, and achieve goals	Develops a collaborative culture to mobilize community resources to support student achievement, solve problems, and achieve goals
Uses school and community resources and social service agencies effectively	Fails to use school and community resources and social service agencies effectively	Attempts to use school and community resources and social service agencies effectively	Actively uses school and community resources and social service agencies effectively	Develops a collaborative culture to use school and community resources and social service agencies effectively
Advocates for resources (financial, human, material, professional development, training, and time) to meet the needs of all learners	Fails to advocate for resources (financial, human, material, professional development, training, and time) to meet the needs of all learners	Attempts to advocate for resources (financial, human, material, professional development, training, and time) to meet the needs of all learners	Actively advocates for resources (financial, human, material, professional development, training, and time) to meet the needs of all learners	Develops a collaborative culture that advocates for resources (financial, human, material, professional development, training, and time) to meet the needs of all learners

(continued)

Table 6.2. *(continued)*

4b. Demonstrates understanding of educational policy	*Level of Performance*			
Element	*Ineffective*	*Initiating*	*Developing*	*Effective*
Understands, responds to, and influences the larger political, social, economic, legal, and cultural context	Fails to understand, respond to, and influence the larger political, social, economic, legal, and cultural context	Attempts to understand, respond to, and influence the larger political, social, economic, legal, and cultural context	Actively understands, responds to, and influences the larger political, social, economic, legal, and cultural context	Develops a collaborative culture that understands, responds to, and influences the larger political, social, economic, legal, and cultural context
Considers and evaluates the potential moral and legal consequences of decision making	Fails to consider and evaluate the potential moral and legal consequences of decision making	Attempts to consider and evaluate the potential moral and legal consequences of decision making	Actively considers and evaluates the potential moral and legal consequences of decision making	Develops a collaborative culture that considers and evaluates the potential moral and legal consequences of decision making
Builds bridges with administration and stakeholders to advance policies that influence quality instruction and student achievement	Fails to build bridges with administration and stakeholders to advance policies that influence quality instruction and student achievement	Attempts to build bridges with administration and stakeholders to advance policies that influence quality instruction and student achievement	Actively builds bridges with administration and stakeholders to advance policies that influence quality instruction and student achievement	Develops a collaborative culture that builds bridges with administration and stakeholders to advance policies that influence quality instruction and student achievement
Steps up and out of classroom to serve at school, district, state, or national levels to shape and implement policy	Fails to step up and out of classroom to serve at school, district, state, or national levels to shape and implement policy	Attempts to step up and out of classroom to serve at school, district, state, or national levels to shape and implement policy	Draws upon resources to step up and out of classroom to serve at school, district, state, or national levels to shape and implement policy	Models and provides resources to step up and out of classroom to serve at school, district, state, or national levels to shape and implement policy

4c. Supports local initiatives	*Level of Performance*			
Element	*Ineffective*	*Initiating*	*Developing*	*Effective*
Creates and supports organizational change	Fails to create and support organizational change	Attempts to create and support organizational change	Actively creates and supports organizational change	Develops a collaborative culture that creates and supports organizational change
Models accountability and responsibility	Fails to model accountability and responsibility	Attempts to model accountability and responsibility	Actively models accountability and responsibility	Develops a collaborative culture that models accountability and responsibility
Collaborates with stakeholders to ensure learner growth and advancement of the profession	Fails to collaborate with stakeholders to ensure learner growth and advancement of the profession	Attempts to collaborate with stakeholders to ensure learner growth and advancement of the profession	Actively collaborates with stakeholders to ensure learner growth and advancement of the profession	Develops a collaborative culture with stakeholders to ensure learner growth and advancement of the profession
Adheres with fidelity to the evaluation process in accordance with role/s	Fails to adhere with fidelity to the evaluation process in accordance with role/s	Attempts to adhere with fidelity to the evaluation process in accordance with role/s	Advocates for and adheres with fidelity to the evaluation process in accordance with role/s	Advances leadership capacity in helping colleagues understand and adhere with fidelity to the evaluation process in accordance with role/s

explore data, research alternatives and provide unbiased recommendations. Personal opinions and politics are removed from the decision-making process to reflect the needs of the community and students who are served. The findings are not to the isolation of one classroom, nor held closely as an individual possession. Rather, these findings are shared across the district, with other districts, and across other entities that may benefit.

4c: Supports Local Initiatives

Finally, Effective teacher leaders *support local initiatives*, the third component of *advocacy*. Local initiatives, often conceptualized as organizational change, are challenging. But Effective teacher leaders recognize the importance of both initiating change and supporting change. They work diligently to encourage a culture that supports change, but that also assesses the effectiveness of that change in the spirit of accountability and responsibility.

Effective teacher leaders know that central to any change is learner growth, and they look for change to impact student learning whether it is a change that originated with them or with others. In modeling and encouraging their own continued learning along with this collaborative spirit, teacher leaders set the tone and pace for the educational community in which they live and work. As teacher leaders model and encourage support for new initiatives, they overcome inertia and initiate momentum that not only affects student learning, but also advances leadership capacity and the profession.

For example, a Developing teacher leader may launch a method to address a critical school initiative, but as importantly, phase out one that was not proving successful for various groups. This can be achieved through several channels such as the virtue of one's own learning; listening to others; gathering data from peers; or engaging in new methodologies and sharing that learning with her peers and supervisors. By raising awareness, trying new methods to address the curricular initiatives, and collecting student impact data, the goals of students are met and a school initiative is advanced.

APPLICATIONS OF *THE FRAMEWORK*

Coaching, Mentoring, Supervision, and *The Framework*

Levels of performance of Ineffective, Initiating, Developing, and Effective teacher leaders are found in the preceding rubrics provided for domains 1 and 4. Using the rubric framework, teacher leaders hone their leadership skills and expertise over time through ongoing professional learning, reflective practice, constructive feedback, and effective mentoring, coaching, and supervision. Like teachers and administrators, teacher leaders always strive for a high level of effective expertise within the arena of their complex work.

Since experience is not the same as expertise, the amount of time on the job does not automatically equate to improvement of leadership ability. Rather, accomplishment is related to setting goals and seeking to learn and grow using the elements and rubrics, as well as the descriptors to scaffold more and more effective skills in all areas of *The Framework for Effective Teacher Leadership*. Mentors, coaches, and supervisors play an important role in guiding teacher leader reflection and goal setting by providing meaningful feedback.

Within *The Framework for Effective Teacher Leadership* rubric, the identifiers of *levels of performance* are consistent throughout all domains. These ratings (Ineffective, Initiating, Developing, and Effective) identify the levels of performance of the teacher leader at that specific point in time. This is significant as it reflects the variability of performance over time and identifies patterns of behavior. Seasoned supervisors and thoughtful coaches and mentors can assist teacher leaders to see their behavior patterns and use the patterns to strengthen their leadership skills.

Additionally, *The Framework for Effective Teacher Leadership* assists in identifying areas of strengths, as well as challenges. Identifying strengths and weaknesses can assist the teacher leader in setting goals. Most importantly, these levels of performance should be used as a tool for professional growth, as well as a platform for professional conversation and critical, specific feedback.

Effective Supervision, Constructive Evaluation, and *The Framework*

Ineffective: A leader performing at the Ineffective level does not yet demonstrate evidence of basic concepts and skills of the component. An Ineffective level of performance can stem from a multitude of reasons including but not limited to:

- little to no understanding
- lack of prerequisite knowledge
- level of error or lack of correction of error
- lack of awareness, responsiveness, or experience
- does not indicate movement to expand one's professional skillset
- placement in a position without necessary experience or training

Professional conversation is also imperative to explore the core reason(s) for an Ineffective rating. It is the responsibility of the evaluator or supervisor to guide the plan for teacher leader improvement with the leader and to set in place the opportunities for coaching and mentoring. Professional conversation and the development of specific professional learning goal(s) would be expected to occur and be implemented in order for the teacher leader to provide evidence of positive growth in the future. Specific timelines and evidence of growth within the plan are essential.

Initiating: A leader performing at the Initiating level appears to have an understanding of the elements of the competent teacher leader, but demonstrates inconsistent implementation and application of the skills or knowledge. The Initiating level reflects the novice teacher leader who is experiencing some of the leadership experiences for the first time. It is commonly due to lack of experience that the teacher leader may identify with the Initiating level.

The evaluator/supervisor of a teacher leader at the Initiating level is encouraged to implement a coaching or mentoring model to achieve positive results of professional growth. Working with the Initiating teacher leader in a supportive, yet focused, environment will provide the foundation for improved performance, and improved leadership skills and dispositions.

Developing: The leader performing at the Developing level has a solid understanding of the elements of the competent teacher leader, and demonstrates the ability to articulate and execute the appropriate leadership skills and/or interactions consistently with a high level of success. This level of competency is noted by others in the organization. The teacher leader is proficient, and has the capacity and skills to change course and seamlessly move to an alternate implementation plan if necessary.

Teacher leaders at the Developing level work to continually improve their practice and members of their professional community seek them out to serve as coaches and mentors. The evaluator/supervisor of a Developing teacher leader would be encouraged to be supportive of the leadership efforts and provide an appropriate platform for continued growth and success.

Effective: The teacher leader performing at the Effective level is a master of the craft. The Effective teacher leader consistently performs at the highest level with high levels of success. This level of teacher leadership is qualitatively and quantitatively different than those of colleagues. The Effective teacher leader is a contributor to the school, community, and professional community.

Once achieving an Effective level of performance does not imply a permanent rating. It is more realistic to move in and out of this distinguished area as the leadership role shifts and grows. It is also possible to not achieve the rating of Effective in all elements at the same time. The evaluator/supervisor of an Effective teacher leader is encouraged to be a champion of the leader's efforts and accomplishments.

SUMMARY

In this chapter, we discuss domains 1 and 4 of *The Framework for Effective Teacher Leadership*. The components of each domain are discussed as well as the elements. Examples provide further clarification. Readers are encouraged to use *The Framework* as a means of identifying and defining a plan of action for growth and development as an effective teacher leader. Domain 1 lays out the foundations of teacher leadership and identifies *critical competencies* while domain 4 suggests a path for growing as a teacher leader and developing *advocacy*.

Critical competencies permeate all aspects of teacher leadership while *advocacy* focuses on one aspect of teacher leadership that an Effective teacher leader develops. Finally, the rubrics suggest a growth pattern that allows teacher leaders to reflect on their strengths and needs and talk about and outline a plan for professional growth. The rubrics can be used to guide mentors, coaches, supervisors, and evaluators as they work with teacher leaders to advance their leadership skills and guide their professional growth.

SELF-ASSESSMENT AND REFLECTION

1. Using the matrix for domain 1, consider your *critical competencies* for effective teacher leadership. What are your strengths? What are your needs? Then consider your current role and identify opportunities to address those competencies. Develop a plan for your professional growth for domain 1.
2. Review the components and elements of *advocacy*. Use the rubrics to identify your strengths and needs in each area. How might you grow as an effective teacher leader in the *advocacy* domain?

REFERENCES

Amabile, T. M., and Kramer, S. J. (2011, May). The power of small wins. *Harvard Business Review 89*(5).

Andrews, H. A. (2011). Supporting quality teaching with recognition. *Australian Journal of Teacher Education 36*(12). Retrieved at http://dx.doi.org/10.14221/ajte.2011v36n12.5

Council of Chief State School Officers. (2015). Interstate School Leaders Licensure Consortium (ISLLC) 2015: Model Policy Standards for Educational Leaders. Washington DC: Council of Chief State School Officers.

Danielson, C. (2007). *Enhancing professional practice: A framework for teaching*. Alexandria, VA: Association for Supervision and Curriculum Development.

———. (2007). The many faces of leadership. *Educational Leadership 65*(1): 14–19.

Grady, M. P., Helbling, K. C., and Lubeck, D. R. (2008). Teacher professionalism since *A Nation at Risk. Phi Delta Kappan 89*, 603–04, 607.

Khalifa, M., Gooden, M., and Davis, J. (2016, December). Culturally responsive school leadership: A synthesis of the literature. *Review of Educational Research 86*(4): 1272–1311.

Teacher Leadership Exploratory Consortium. (2008). Teacher leader model standards. Washington, DC: National Education Association (NEA).

Tomlinson, C. A. (2014). *The differentiated classroom: Responding to the needs of all learners.* Alexandria, VA: Association for Supervision and Curriculum Development.

Chapter Seven

Professional Learning to Enhance Teacher Leadership

OBJECTIVES

Throughout this chapter you will:

1. Identify the cyclical process (TLMS 3; NELP 4; PESL 4,5,6 and 7; NBPTS 4, 5).
2. Examine types of professional learning and growth (TLMS 3; NELP 7; PESL 7; NBPTS 4, 5).
3. Investigate differentiated professional learning (TLMS 6; NELP 2; PESL 2; NBPTS 4, 5).
4. Examine professional learning and self-renewal (TLMS 7; NELP 6; PESL6; NBPTS 4, 5).

THE CYCLICAL PROCESS

Often teacher leaders begin their new role with little or no preparation. The thought process is if a teacher is effective in the classroom, then why not as a leader? But just as teachers and principals need professional development, so do teacher leaders. Professional development as defined by the National Staff Development Council (NSDC 2018, p. 1) is:

> *A comprehensive, sustained, and intensive approach to improving teachers' and principals' effectiveness in raising student achievement. Effective professional development is aligned to rigorous state and local standards and priorities, job-embedded, facilitated by experts and based on a model of continuous*

improvement, and should directly impact a teacher's classroom practices and student achievement.

As with teachers and principals, professional development for teacher leaders is ongoing. There is an expectation for continuous improvement that is cyclical, meaning that the process is a series of events that once completed begins again in the same order, building on the results of the previous process.

Historically this idea of continuous improvement was launched in industry with the work of W. Edward Deming who advanced the Fourteen Points of Quality Assurance (Deming 1986). Essentially, Deming called for a cycle of *plan, do, check, and take action*. Wiggins and McTighe (2007) adapted this cycle for educators to include vision, feedback, and adjust.

This concept of professional-development cycle describes the learning process for teacher leaders. Thus, teacher leaders are the leading learners and engage in professional learning in order to acquire the knowledge, skills, dispositions, and depth of understanding necessary to drive systemic change in addition to their personal development.

We believe that the distinction between professional development and professional learning matters. According to Learning Forward (2011), standards for *professional learning* include learning communities, leadership, resources, learning designs, implementation, and outcomes. Standards such as these delineate conditions, processes, and content of professional learning.

Are professional development and professional learning one and the same? No, and the distinction is an important one for teacher leaders. Development connotes something that someone does to something or someone else with a specific end in mind. For example, land developers build housing or commercial buildings, photographers develop film, or weightlifters develop strong muscles.

Learning, however, is much more. While some learning does enable teacher leaders to build specific skills, the learning process is often more important than the skill because of what they learn about themselves, their schools, and their communities when they apply the knowledge and skills they've acquired. Teacher leaders learn that feedback often shapes final outcomes, and that they continue to learn even as they lead.

Learning requires ownership, and a deep personal investment of self and one's time (and often money). Therefore, professional learning is a more apt nomenclature as the role of the teacher leader seeks to acquire the necessary knowledge, skills, and habits of mind to make broad, lasting changes and not just develop their own teaching and leading abilities. In fact, it is the professional learning that leads to personal development that in turn enables one to be a more effective leader, and with this growth comes self-renewal.

Unlike the pendulum of professional development for principals that has swung from school management to instructional leadership, the focus for teacher leaders has always centered around student learning. In the era of the Every Student Succeeds Act, the cycle for professional learning for teacher leaders revolves around improving their abilities to utilize information and data-based decision making within specific contexts to improve student learning—learning specific to a group of students in a particular community with specific needs and access to particular opportunities and resources.

The cycle includes: *assess, prioritize and set goals, identify resources, act, evaluate outcomes and reflect. Assess* refers to examining the needs of the teacher leader. Sometimes a teacher leader will have a supervisor who will assess them, but effective teacher leaders often self-assess and see many needs within their own classroom, grade level, department, or school.

Some needs will be more immediate for the teacher leader and the context in which the teacher leader is working; therefore, the teacher leader will have to prioritize needs and set goals. For example, using *The Framework for Effective Teacher Leadership*, the skills in domain 1 are foundational and, therefore, critical to address in order to acquire and develop more complex skills.

The teacher leader sets goals and identifies resources to draw upon both internally, with mentors, coaches, and peers, and externally with college and university faculty, courses, conferences, and programs. Upon accessing critical resources to address the goal and need identified, the teacher leader creates a plan for his or her professional learning and growth.

Ideally, as a lead learner, the teacher leader's plan includes an array of related experiences ranging from immersive, interactive activities, to thorough and close readings of relevant research, to traditional courses and workshops. As a lead learner, the successful teacher leader seeks out coaches or mentors to support both the learning experiences and the application of such within the school.

Critical to the cycle of learning for all teacher leaders is evaluation and reflection. What was learned? Was the goal met? Was the intended learning met? If not, what are the current needs and what revisions need to be made? If so, how has this been shared, and how will what was learned assist the teacher leader to address a new need and set next goals? What evidence is available to substantiate effective implementation? What data were used, and was use of this data effective?

TYPES OF PROFESSIONAL LEARNING AND GROWTH

For teacher leaders, professional learning is often job embedded. This doesn't necessarily mean that teacher leaders only learn on the job; rather, needs and goals often come from work in the classroom or school. Conversely, the learning associated with this professional development is often applied with teachers, classrooms or schools—in other words, the learning is applied in the places where teacher leaders work and in spaces where decisions about teaching and learning occur.

In all cases of teacher leader learning, leaders are reflective as was described in the cyclical process of learning for teacher leaders. Reflective practice, as described by Schon (1983), is taken a step further here to not only refer to teachers looking at student learning to improve their own practice, but to teacher leaders reflecting on the impact of their leadership skills on their colleagues and ultimately student learning.

Sometimes that reflection may be framed by other administrators and sometimes it may be teacher leaders themselves that drive the reflection, but either way *The Framework of Teacher Leadership* may be used to outline skills and knowledge to advance teacher leadership. Similarly, *The Framework of Teacher Leadership* could be used to coach or mentor a teacher leader.

Coaching occurs best in situations where a culture for shared leadership has been established with a strong element of trust. Principals, assistant principals, and department chairs trust teachers and teacher leaders to be good thinkers and problem-solvers in and out of the classroom while teachers and teacher leaders trust their supervisors to back their risk-taking and innovations all to improve student learning.

When something fails, then, it is not seen as a punishable offense, but rather a moment from which to learn. Principals, department chairs, or assistant principals may serve as coaches to teacher leaders. As such, teacher leaders will use their coaches as sounding boards not only to listen to and provide feedback, but to guide problem-solving, ask questions, and provide formative assessment. In addition to trust, critical to the success of coaching is time—regularly scheduled time to work together to refine skills and assess progress toward achieving targeted goals.

Mentoring, like coaching, may rely on tools such as *The Framework for Teacher Leadership*, and likewise, a relationship of trust is of the utmost importance. Though somewhat more informal than coaching, trust must be a critical factor in the successful relationship between mentor and mentee so that the teacher leader feels comfortable sharing challenges, fears, and mis- or lack of understandings as well as celebrating successes.

Mentors for teacher leaders may be more experienced colleagues, retired teachers, or even revered college or university faculty. The focus in mentoring is on improving reflection and building confidence so it is important for teacher leaders to identify a mentor who can listen and discuss matters in such a way as to help guide reflection and build self-efficacy.

For example, one teacher leader who was leading an initiative in implementing social emotional learning chose to work with a mentor who recently retired. The teacher was having difficulty convincing her colleagues to incorporate the Social and Emotional Learning (SEL) standards into the teaching day because several perceived it as an add-on rather than something to integrate into regular instruction.

Working with a retired teacher who understood the culture of the school and potential flash points of the system, the teacher leader learned how to gather evidence and who to share it with first. In biweekly meetings, the mentor was able to help the teacher leader identify potential landmines and coach specifically to create effective presentations to grade levels and the staff. Over time, most of the staff came to realize the value of the social emotional integration and incorporate it into their regular instruction.

Using action research for professional development allows teacher leaders to put legs to their best ideas, as well as give wings if they find that it works. Less formal than scientific research, an action research process enables teacher leaders to pursue a particular idea, intervention, or even a hunch that a particular action will lead to a specific outcome as well as to additional unanticipated outcomes. The action research process includes identifying and articulating a problem, creating multiple possible solutions, choosing and implementing one that the teacher leader thinks will be most successful, collecting data, analyzing the information gleaned from the data, and sharing the results.

For example, one sixth-grade teacher leader believed the class was too fidgety and would do better sitting on exercise balls than in chairs. Coupled with support from the PTA, exercise balls were purchased to replace chairs. Colleagues observed the changes as well as being captured in real time and on videotape, corroborating boys bounced and rolled on the exercise balls frequently. Also noted was that students were able to pay more attention, and the need to discipline students for annoying behaviors such as poking and teasing decreased significantly. This classroom became more productive and pleasant.

Action research may or may not involve a mentor or coach, but it always involves reflection. Reflection is central to the analysis, but hard data is even more central to reflection in action research as it may be used to support a policy change, or at the very least be shared with others as what works.

What is essential in using action research as professional development is the idea with which the teacher leader begins, and the support or lack of support found for the original idea in the outcome. Does it work? To what extent has it worked? What went well? What are the challenges or barriers? What needs to be changed, and how? How powerful is the evidence?

DIFFERENTIATED PROFESSIONAL LEARNING

All students do not benefit equally well from the same instruction. Why would we assume professional learning would be any different for teachers, principals, or teacher leaders? Teacher leaders are learners and often the lead learners in their schools. They benefit most from personalized learning that best fits their identified needs and priorities. For example, the teacher leader who is an expert in project-based learning will likely not benefit from a district-wide introductory workshop on this topic.

Therefore, there must be flexibility and choice to better serve teacher leaders. Options allow teacher leaders to pursue a learning experience related to a more specific, relevant, and needed component such as how to measure the impact of project-based learning, or how to influence organizational change in order to support colleagues' first attempts at using it. Consequently, teacher leaders need to work with their own supervisors to negotiate opportunities to pursue a more personalized path of professional development than might ordinarily be available.

PROFESSIONAL LEARNING AND SELF-RENEWAL

At a time when more and more is demanded of schools and principals, the role of teacher leader becomes increasingly important. At the same time, however, most states are facing a teacher shortage in the near future and the pool for potential teacher leaders is dwindling even as we read this book. Why? The most frequent reasons given for teachers leaving the profession are negative working conditions including relationships with principals; overwhelming demands without requisite support; opportunities to collaborate, grow, and develop; opportunities for career pathways; salary and benefits; and school safety.

A teacher leader can be instrumental in providing the support necessary to decrease attrition and arguably to enhance recruitment of new teachers. The teacher leader can be an intermediary for relations with a principal, and provide support for handling particular problems that may overwhelm a teacher, whether implementing a new curriculum or assisting in managing a difficult parent. Teacher leaders foster collaboration, and the presence of the role in the school is tangible evidence of a commitment to a career pathway.

Teacher leaders, however, face similar issues with working conditions and must be afforded time and funding for continuous learning and their own self-renewal. Too often, districts restrict travel for teacher leaders because of financial limitations. Teacher leaders should be encouraged to attend and to present at conferences in order to learn new ways to support teachers and share success stories that ultimately enhance the district's attractiveness for future teachers. Funding teacher leaders' professional learning is an essential investment in the school and district's future. As with any successful investment, the long-term growth far outweighs the short-term expense.

Teacher leaders not only need continuous learning opportunities to support their schools but also for their own self-renewal. Making time for keeping current with new research, learning about innovative methods and materials, and connecting with other teacher leaders not only gives insights into how they can better serve their schools but also time to think and reflect on their own practices. Learning opportunities makes them better leaders and renews their commitment and enthusiasm. With firsthand learning experiences, teacher leaders are both more eager and better equipped to lead important changes.

For example, one high school wanted to explore changing from a traditional schedule to a full-block schedule. While the principal and district fully supported this plan, most teachers were at best wary of it and more than a few opposed it. The district wisely invested in providing ample release time and adequate funding for the teacher leader team to learn about the pros and cons, the costs and benefits, and the nuances of various types of block schedules. Teacher leaders visited other schools, connected with colleagues in other schools that had recently made a similar change, and read voraciously.

Over the course of just ten weeks, the teacher leaders developed a renewed energy and commitment for moving to a block schedule. They experienced a deep sense of self-renewal after realizing how much their students and teachers would benefit from the change and knowing that the success of the planned change depended on their ability to share their learning with the more recalcitrant faculty.

In the end, their excitement generated from their learning and self-renewal moved the majority of the staff. They were able to make an authentic, compelling case for the block schedule and to engage colleagues by sharing their own learning experiences. The block schedule became a reality because of teacher leaders' opportunities for learning and self-renewal.

While the working conditions affecting teacher attrition pose challenges, they also offer opportunities to create environments that build capacity for teacher leadership and student success. Using tools for teacher growth and development like *The Framework for Effective Teacher Leadership*, providing space and resources for that development to occur, acknowledging the contributions teacher leaders have on school success, and assuring opportunities for continuous learning and self-renewal foster the conditions necessary for professional educators to thrive and to drive school improvement.

SUMMARY

The focus in chapter 7 is on professional development, or rather professional learning differentiated in terms of the important role the teacher leader plays in the process of growth and development. However, in many ways much of this entire book focuses on professional learning since it carves out and describes in detail a scaffold for thinking about growing as a teacher leader using *The Framework for Teacher Leadership.* For example, in chapter 6, you learn about domain 1 and its elements and components, and you see how learned 1 provides a conduit from effective teaching to teacher leadership. Similarly, in chapter 5, you learn about growing as an instructional coach.

Critical in the understanding of teacher leader professional learning using any domain is the notion that professional learning is differentiated to fit the teacher leader as well as reflect experiences, context, and resources. In all cases, professional learning is autonomous. It is the teacher leader who controls professional learning and likewise, it is the teacher leader who is accountable for that learning.

Professional learning for teacher leaders may take on many forms including coaching, mentoring, book studies, action research, and course completion but in all cases it is job related. Either the need to learn comes from the leader's work, the leader uses new learning to enhance or improve work, or both. In addition to what is brought to the leader's work, the experience of integrating something new or modified at work generates professional learning.

Central to all professional learning is reflection. While teacher leaders may meet with supervisors for evaluation, get feedback from coaches, share in discussions with mentors, or take classes with college faculty, it is the teacher leader who ultimately must analyze the input from each human resource, filter and synthesize it with accumulated knowledge, experience, and knowledge of context, and take action.

Once taken, those leadership decisions and actions are reflected on and produce opportunities for additional or deeper learning. Professional learning is continuous, and reflection is a key component of the process of growth and development that lead to student achievement and school success.

SELF-ASSESSMENT AND REFLECTION

1. Describe the best ways you learn and grow as a leader. Are you engaging in professional development or professional learning?
2. What are the opportunities for you to engage in professional learning as a teacher leader? In what form(s) of professional development do you regularly participate?

3. How can you maximize the opportunities in your school or district to grow and develop as a teacher leader? What could your school or district do to enhance your growth and development as a teacher leader? What role might you play in making those ideas a reality? What resources can be tapped, or whom might you need to have that conversation with to pursue additional resources?

REFERENCES

Deming, W. E. (1986). *Out of crisis*. Boston, MA: MIT Press.

Learning Forward. (2011). *Standards for professional learning*. Oxford, OH: Learning Forward.

National Staff Development Council. (2018). Proposal to amend: Elementary and secondary education act of 1965 (ESEA). Title IX. Section 9101 (34). Retrieved from http://aypf.org/documents/62609NSDCDefinitionofProfessionalDevelopment908.pdf

Schon, D. (1983). *The reflective practitioner*. New York: Basic Books.

Wiggins, G. and McTighe, J. (2007). *Schooling by design: Mission, action and achievement*. Alexandria, VA: Association for Supervision and Curriculum Development.

Chapter Eight

The Research Behind *The Framework for Effective Teacher Leadership*

OBJECTIVES

Throughout this chapter you will:

1. Examine assumptions and attributes of *The Framework* (PSEL 2, 3, 4, 5, 8, 9, 10; NELP 1–7; NBPTS 5; MTLS 1-7)
2. Review findings and limitations (PSEL 2, 6, 8, 10; NELP 7; NBPTS 4; MTLS 2, 3, 4, 5).
3. Review an analysis, synthesis, and evaluation of the data (PSEL 10; NELP 7; NBPTS 4; MTLS 2, 3, 4, 5).
4. Consider recommendations for the future (PSEL 2, 3, 6, 10; NELP 2-7; NBPTS 4, 5; MTLS 2, 5)

ASSUMPTIONS AND ATTRIBUTES OF *THE FRAMEWORK*

The Framework for Effective Teacher Leadership represents all aspects of the daily work expected of those serving, formally or informally, in teacher leader roles whether implicitly or explicitly stated. *The Framework* has both theoretical and conceptual frameworks that have led to its development. It is anchored in a multitude of standards reflective of expectations of reputable educational organizations.

Assumptions of *The Framework*

A framework such as Danielson's (2013) *Framework for Teaching* provides foundational expectations of the classroom teacher. Demonstrating knowledge of content and pedagogy, setting instructional outcomes, and such reflect the complexity of teaching. With the additional skill sets and processes developed as a teacher leader, acquisition of such skills and depth of knowledge moves the teacher leader along a continuum of growth and professional learning. The teacher leader outgrows the *Framework for Teaching* yet roles, responsibilities, and interests make leadership resources inapplicable.

While the intent of *The Framework for Effective Teacher Leadership* is for professional growth and development, evaluation must be addressed. By keeping teacher leaders on a teacher evaluation or evaluating them as an administrator, teacher leaders have been misplaced. Therefore, it is critical to have a tool that is relevant to skill sets and processes specific to teacher leaders.

Learning is organic, meaning the need, desire, or interest to develop the intellectual capacity to acquire, process, and apply information changes. On any given day, a particular combination of factors can determine a need, a change of direction, or a change of events. The *Framework* provides flexibility to the user to identify initial placement, movement back and forth along the continuum, and the ability to meet the needs of the teacher leader if not all components or elements are currently applicable.

The Framework offers a comprehensive resource outlining a framework specific to the knowledge, skills, dispositions, and practices of teacher leaders. Development of such a framework provides clear expectations, identification of levels of performance (rubrics), placement on a continuum, and accountability of growth.

Teaching is a noble profession with many pathways. While sometimes thought of as a flat profession, districts have moved from a step-and-lane career ladder approach to a multiple pathway lattice approach. With a career ladder, it could be wrongfully concluded that since teacher leaders are purposefully opting to lead from the classroom, they are in a middle rung and will never reach the top; however, this couldn't be further from the truth, since the purpose of teacher leadership is to transform knowledge, skills, dispositions, and practices of effective teacher leaders to impact student learning, colleagues, and the district and school.

Attributes of *The Framework*

The Framework embodies a number of attributes that demonstrate its validity and applicability to a wide range of settings. At the national level there must be an understanding of the interrelatedness of supervision, evaluation, and professional learning and growth. The call for voice must be answered and not left an empty request. It is crucial to advocate and make connections with lawmakers at all levels to educate those not in the classrooms, as well as direct and support legislation that will positively impact classrooms around the nation.

At the state level, recognition of teacher leaders has resulted in endorsement and licensure. Also statewide, partnerships with institutions of higher education has led to formal training through recognized, accredited programs or degrees. Again, voice, connections with lawmakers, and advocacy for colleagues and students are fundamental to change.

At the local level, recognition of teacher leaders presented the need for school districts and school leaders to define this tier of leadership, recognize roles held by teacher leaders, identify skills sets and processes exemplified by this group, and determine how they will be evaluated. In addition to a call for a resource for evaluation that allows teacher leaders to demonstrate proficiency, *The Framework* provides a continuum and common language for teacher leaders to create goals to promote growth within a structure that reflects inter-rater reliability.

Effective teacher leadership calls for understanding and appropriately and acceptably implementing shared or distributed leadership by building- and district-level administration, and defining, adhering to, and supporting accountability measures by both administration and the Boards that oversee them. For teacher leaders to continue to grow and impact those around them, they must conduct action research in a culture that exemplifies freedom, support, and risk-taking.

The Framework is grounded in empirical, theoretical, and conceptual research. The empirical research is grounded in experience and observation. Theoretical and conceptual research reflect theories, strategies, standards, competencies, and propositions specific to teaching, leadership, and teacher leadership. *The Framework* is comprehensive in that it encompasses *all* of teacher leadership. *The Framework* is organized in a nonredundant manner, so each domain, each component and each element represents distinct knowledge, skills, dispositions, or practices of teacher leadership. From the classroom, to the school, to the district, to the state, to our nation's capital, we have *The Framework* as a guide.

The Framework is coherent and intentional. The language of *The Framework* was carefully chosen through a process of examination and categorization of standards crossing teaching (NBPTS), leadership (PSEL and NELP), and specifically teacher leadership (MTLS). The verbs in both *The Framework* and the corresponding rubrics were carefully chosen to represent the desired action as well as valid evidence. If the purpose of the tool is for professional growth, then goal setting, analysis of practice, and improvement are the focus. If the purpose of the tool is for evaluation, the teacher leader must identify observable and analyzed (not anticipated or intended) practice supported by evidence.

FINDINGS AND LIMITATIONS

Findings of the Survey

Key findings from this study include confirmation that data collected is consistent with data collected and reviewed in prior studies. In other words, what was problematic before remains problematic. One observation made during analysis is that the number of participants answering the question dropped as the questions became more specific to impact, policy, and voice. Participation was higher when the participant merely reported procedures such as roles or selection. Survey questions are located in appendix A.

Roles of teacher leaders are identified by the US Department of Education (Ed.Gov) as mentor/coach, leadership team member, department chair, lead teacher, curriculum specialist, instructional specialist, and policy leader. The survey showed that the assumed roles of teacher leaders as well as appointed roles, as shown in table 8.1.

Exploring the structural implications of teacher leadership, nearly half of the respondents reported the role of teacher leaders in their school as formal while the other half reported the role as informal with teachers emerging into these teacher leader roles. Only half of the respondents confirmed there to be a job description available for these roles, and even fewer confirmed there to be a clearly defined evaluation process. This section of the survey confirmed

Table 8.1. US DoE, Assumed and Appointed Roles

Teacher Leader Roles as Identified by the US Department of Education:	*Assumed Roles Percentages (Data Gathered Via Survey of Teacher Leaders):*	*Appointed Roles Percentages (Data Gathered Via Survey of Teacher Leaders):*
Mentor/Coach • Leadership Team Member • Department Chair • Lead Teacher	Mentoring 65.63% Team Lead/Grade Level 62.5%	Mentoring 75% Team Lead/Grade Level 65.63%
• Instructional Specialist • Curriculum Specialist	• Instructional Coach 53.13% • Data Coach 43.75% Voice in Decision Making 50%	• Instructional Coach 62% • Data Coach 50%
		Professional Development Organizer 46.88%
Policy Leader	Union Representative 43.75%	Union Representative 40.63%

there are clearly defined knowledge, skills, dispositions, and practices that a teacher leader must exhibit, and that teacher leaders have the ear of their administration as well as the allocated resources to act within the role.

Exploring the cultural implications of teacher leadership, the numbers were very favorable in all areas but one: collaboration. Reportedly, some teacher leaders exhibit this skill and bring teams together, while others take credit for the work of the group. On the flipside, an area where all participants agreed teacher leaders positively impacted school culture was advocating for students. Other areas identified as having positive impact were student learning, encouraging others to take risks and propose new ideas, and being valued as a professional.

Specific to selection of teacher leaders, areas identified by all respondents showed those serving in such roles are open to input and feedback, are collaborative, and work well with both administrators and teachers. Other areas identified include reflective practices, transparency, ethical practices, and demonstrate self-knowledge. The areas that were low in this section were that the actual selection process was known, and the criteria for selection was known indicating that communication, policy, and procedure might need to be addressed.

This is confirmed in the next section of the survey, specific to trends. This section showed that teacher leaders are reportedly not recognized by the respondents' state through licensure, certification or endorsement. Furthermore, respondents reported lack of shared standards for teacher leaders at the district level; lack of communication provided by the state or district specific to teacher leadership; lack of specific guidelines, policy, or procedures specific to teacher leadership; and lack of structure and allocated resources to support teacher leaders. However, teacher leaders were reported as active participants in strategic planning; data collection, analysis and reporting; and student achievement.

The influences or reasons teachers move into teacher leadership were ranked. At the top of the list were students and building leaders. Other influences ranked high were professional development/training, personal experience, colleagues, and curriculum. Perceptions of participants specific to US Department of Education were mostly *don't know* on the Likert scale, indicating that respondents are unaware of the functions and support. State departments, district leadership, and building leadership were viewed as supportive. Local boards of education were viewed as supportive but not as favorable. Unions, colleagues, higher education institutions, and nonprofits had positive perceptions by the respondents.

When asked about limitations placed on teacher leaders, and by whom, two responses recurred: time and voice. Time in that respondents reported the need to work with others, try new strategies, and engage in reflection without the conflicting district initiatives stealing time. Voice in that respondents reported either not having voice in policy and decision making as that was left to the administration, or sharing voice but not having it implemented. Other limitations include teacher leaders not having a place in the district vision; budgetary confines, specifically personnel; systemic support including finances and personnel; understanding one's role; and colleagues.

The accountability section of the survey was an open-ended question that generated a variance of responses. Accountability was viewed as sharing information with the group; translating policies, reforms, and initiatives; keeping the team on target; facilitating collaborative planning agendas; leading data sessions; and proving clear, detailed communication systems, agendas, and plans. Here one of the respondents captured teacher leaders' accountability in this way, "Take responsibility for department setbacks, but give credit to the staff for accomplishments."

Teacher leaders create and support change through professional development and training, curriculum development, and leading teams (PLC, grade level, SIP, etc.). They also collaborate to create formative assessments, review student progress, support instruction, and provide feedback. Through a wider lens, they model, carry out school-wide goals, and keep focused on providing an equitable education for all students.

Specific characteristics listed by respondents identify teacher leaders as excellent teachers demonstrating knowledge and skills; they have experience in the classroom; demonstrate they are trustworthy, respectful, reflective, professional, relatable, and collaborative; and are risk takers, demonstrate a growth mindset, are student focused, and share voice. A number of other characteristics were identified, such as culturally competent, flexible, courageous, supportive, assertive, unbiased, approachable, and a motivator.

Teacher leaders' impact on collaboration as it affects the culture and climate of the school had two areas that were repeated: bridge or liaisons of collaboration, and keep teachers positive. Other areas identified were to bring new ideas forward, ask the right questions, and find pathways for improvement. This area had some negative connotations, such as the teacher leader being a servant to the principal, teacher leader voice not being implemented, selection of teacher leaders being relational rather than performance based, and there being too many obstacles to make a difference.

Teacher leaders' impact on students is reportedly achieved through mentoring, supporting teachers (coaching), and having a regular presence in walk-throughs. Other areas identified include teaching strategies, creating presentations and modeling, promoting equitable practices and cultural proficiency, and building relational trust.

The use of assessment and data to drive or inform decision making is reported as effectively used to meet students' needs instructionally. In addition, teacher leaders work with colleagues to create formative assessments, collaborate with planning, and try different strategies. Teacher leaders reportedly harness skills and expertise of others through shared ideas, shared lessons, shared professional development, and highlighting celebrations. This section questioned the preparation of teacher leaders not in readiness, but in preparedness to do such tasks as to harness the skills and expertise of others without formal training.

On the larger scale, teacher leaders impact the community around them. teacher leaders see a need, and connect students or families to the resources in the community to meet the need. Whether it is the PTA, a local business, or a local food bank, teacher leaders listen, network, and connect.

Findings of the Focus Groups

The focus groups were discussions specific to teacher leadership. The researcher acted as a facilitator within the group by posing open-ended questions, asking for clarification or examples, or seeking additional information to supplement, support, or further explain the initial response.

The focus groups were also the tool used to obtain feedback on *The Framework for Effective Teacher Leadership*. Participants were provided the initial tool, which featured all standards, competencies, and propositions taken from teacher leader model standards, teacher leadership competencies (Center for Teaching Quality), National Board for Professional Teaching Standards, National Education Association, Educational Leadership Constituent Council, Interstate School Leaders Licensure Consortium, International Coaching Federation, Framework for Effective Leadership (Strike et al. 2016), and *Framework for Effective Teaching* (Danielson 2011).

The focus group was instructed to code by striking or placing a negative sign by components or elements that were not reflective of the work they know of teacher leaders, were beyond the scope of such role, or were repetitive. Furthermore, they were asked to place a plus sign or star those components or elements that captured the roles and responsibilities of teacher leaders, using multiple plus signs, stars, or exclamation points to identify those viewed of more importance. Marginal notes were encouraged.

The initial framework consisted of 4 domains, 15 components, and 108 elements. While the list reflected a compilation of all standards, components, and propositions, the sheer volume makes the collection unattainable by even the best of the best teachers. Therefore, the feedback provided by the focus groups was then used to pare the initial list down to an attainable four domains, fourteen components, and fifty-six elements.

Establishing a framework as a tool for self-assessment, to provide measurable growth, call for evidence, and analyze one's craft was of particular interest within the focus groups. One participant stated the tool is "wide enough to access but specific enough to be helpful."

Concerns with the framework included the fact that it may come to be used for evaluation purposes, and having one's own framework differentiates teachers from teacher leaders, thus creating a divide. An observation from participants in multiple focus-group sessions is that teacher leaders are not *allowed* to do some of the work.

Conversations within the groups focused on the roles and impact of teacher leaders. At the core of the discussions was student achievement. Focus was on motivation, vested interests, home-school partnerships and parent involvement, the culture of the school, barriers to learning, and assessments and how they are used and reported.

Even in the small, impromptu focus groups, teacher leaders shared ideas, asked questions, and networked to bring assistance back to their own buildings: war-room of data, creating stretch goals, parent involvement, teachers in the classroom, asking students about their own learning, creative ways to establish common planning time, strategies to meet the needs of low achievers, and identifying and addressing outside influences that impact the school—you name it, they were on it.

One participant pointed out that it is the core values of the district that lead conversations within the schools. Within multiple focus groups, it was understood that teacher leadership is a progression—a linear continuum that begins with preservice, continues through induction and the novice teacher, and continues to grow through veteran teachers.

Challenges expressed within the focus groups include: lack of position, role or authority; no direction; lots of undeliverables; lack of professional development or training; autonomy; reading the roller-coaster of changes in administration; and differences in salary between teachers and administration, benefits, roles, responsibilities, or no additional pay or stipend for the additional work. In some models shared, teachers were given additional duties as required in their teaching contract under *other duties as assigned*, whereas other teachers were removed from the classroom and made a Teacher on Special Assignment (TSA) while still on a teacher's contract. Stipends sometimes accompany specific roles, such as literacy coach, gifted and talented or positive behavior interventions, and support director. Some participants shared that schools must qualify for teacher leaders. In other words, when they are performing low enough as a school over a set amount of time, then the reinforcements are hired to support the staff.

Findings of the Interviews

The questions posed in the interviews were all open-ended (see appendix B). The interview began with the interviewer asking the participant to share the definition of teacher leadership as used in their school or district. Of the eight respondents, one had a clearly articulated definition and another purposely did not define teacher leadership as a role or position, but through a set of skills. The others had teacher leaders, but no known definition of teacher leadership.

Teacher leadership remains defined by the entity using the term, and there is not a universal, common definition recognized. However, discussions have revealed the reason for this is to allow local districts and schools to utilize teacher leaders as needed in their particular setting to meet their particular needs. Through discussion and interview, there is recognition that once a role, position, or responsibilities are defined, the concept then becomes boxed, and only initiatives or programs that fit in that box are funded; therefore, by not specifically defining teacher leadership, it allows more flexibility to fund such necessary functions. Teacher leadership is not a concept, but a skill set.

The selection of teacher leaders varied greatly. Respondents consistently reported that no additional credentials were necessary (license, endorsement, certification, or coursework) unless one was moving into a specific role; for example, literacy coach, which then required a content-specific license.

Beyond this one area of agreement, respondents reported a gamut from principal recommendation to teachers willing to spend the extra time as ways teachers moved into these positions. In some districts there is a very formal application process; others allow the administrator to nominate or choose teacher leaders based on the type of leadership needed, and others are teachers who have emerged into a more public eye. Most teacher leaders were approved by building level administration without the need for district or board approval; however, some positions, such as content-specific coaches or interventionists, required such approval.

Specific to the relationship between teacher leaders and administrators, one of the participants summed it up by stating that the school's administrator is okay with teacher leadership as long as it happens below the administrator. Other respondents stated there was lack of support from administration, lack of authority of the teacher leaders, or that it varies by building and administrator. While a positive rapport is reported, the effectiveness of teacher leaders is greatly impacted by the leader's support and communication.

In an effort to address this systemic change necessary for effective teacher leadership, one district is putting all faculty and administration through teacher leadership training—together. This way, both groups hear that they have the support of the district, they build up skills of adults, and they understand who is accountable for what, and where to go if this becomes an issue. Support from other districts comes in the form of additional trainings, collaboration time with others, and some additional resources. One district has set aside funds for teacher leader Foundation Grants, which have funded toolkits of instructional strategies for parents, a 3-D printer, and a make-and-take space.

Communication proves to be a challenge, from understanding different communication styles to timely communication. First it must be present, then it must be clear and timely. Learning how to talk *with* someone rather than *at* someone is imperative to those serving in these roles. Listening and actually implementing the recommendations made makes a difference in both perception and future involvement of teacher leaders.

Finally, having discussions at the right time is imperative. For example, approaching teachers as they stand at their door greeting students or are serving bus duty are lost opportunities in that the teachers' attention is divided, and what could have been a productive conversation was untimely. The traits of good communication skills specific to teacher leaders included good listening skills; ability to hear what was said; open; honest; understood the audience; clearly articulated; and held in confidence.

Many examples of the impact of teacher leaders on student achievement were shared. These examples ranged from helping teachers implement new strategies, to modeling being a reflective practitioner. Teacher leaders often facilitate the use of data within teams, and share without shame; model or coteach instructional strategies; encourage and facilitate deeper level conversations; ask probing questions; collaborate with others to share ideas; and support struggling teachers.

Examples of the impact of teacher leaders on colleagues were offered as such: facilitate team meetings; provide opportunities to speak and learn from each other; provide instructional coaching; provide strategies and resources; build rapport through professional relationships; demonstrate all teachers are valued; build trust; speak freely about both positives and negatives, but have potential solutions readily available; plan and show where it can lead; ignite excitement; and celebrate accomplishments of staff and students alike.

Examples of the impact on the school or district include cohesive, universal focus on goals; sharing growth mindset; inclusion in professional development such as a book study; fidelity and evaluation of programs; change, establish or reinforce culture of the school; build morale; and push thinking to contemplate and become action.

While most respondents could retrieve some examples of impact, the next question was specific to sustainable change and rendered responses such as sustainability can happen IF the district maintains those positions and has an open mind, but often district leadership changes direction and teacher leaders aren't provided the time to catch up or change. Several respondents shared changes made by teacher leaders are, indeed, sustainable through time and effort. If made everyday practice, the changes are not viewed in isolation but in totality. If we truly move to shared or distributed leadership, then sustainable change is a collective interest.

Emotion can emerge from the topic of accountability. From principals' perspective, being held accountable for the school building and all that takes place within it can provide a solid argument for wanting or needing to hold on to power. However, micromanaging, noncompliance with the recommendations of the group or making decisions by oneself sends an obvious message that administration and teachers, including teacher leaders, will never work together.

Therefore, it is imperative that there be open, honest, and clear communication specific to roles, responsibilities, and the accountability specific to them from the beginning. This should not change with administrative changes, but be set by the district (or school, based on structure). Participants of the interviews shared that administration sees itself as accountable. If teacher leaders are held accountable, this may be done through a formal teacher evaluation, weekly documents such as agendas and minutes, or random visitations.

Through the lens of collaboration, the respondents identified: the need to have experienced teacher leaders in the classroom; constant conversations; compromise; build consensus; demonstrate oneself as competent and trustworthy; set goals together; create common (formative) assessments; analyze data; make adjustments in instruction, curriculum or practices; search for gaps and plan ways to close them; and recognize the contributions of each member.

When asked what hinders or challenges teacher leaders, or deters others from wanting to take on this role, one area surfaced repeatedly: other teachers. Fear of using one's voice and losing one's job; politics; fear of making a mistake; peers look on teacher leaders negatively; sabotage by colleagues; and professional jealousy were all shared.

Other challenges shared are inability to talk to the higher-ups; teacher leaders viewed as more aggressive because they are more aware; settle and do not want to change or challenge the status quo; difficult to wear different hats and remain part of the faculty; teaching staff does not reflect the population served, or understand the population served; the structure of our schools specific to logistics (schedules, multiple buildings) and time; and time with families is precious.

Celle Beck, curriculum director, Effingham Unit 40 (IL) shared, "Teachers don't really see the value they have on the world. They are pretty beat up . . . through teacher leadership we need to build self-confidence back up because we really do have a lot of incredible educators" (personal communication, January 5, 2018).

When asked what inspires or encourages the teacher leaders within the district or school, the respondents reported wanting to do your best for the kids you service; opportunities kids need and should have; want to excel; power as a collective group versus one; everyone brings strengths to the table; value; voice; ownership; happier; freed to speak; being heard; looking at where we were and where we are now, and being supported as we try new things; see changes in our students both academically and behaviorally—doing them right; being treated as a professional; sharing the mindset that you do whatever it takes; passion—praise, impact, and growth; and possibilities.

Limitations

Limitations varied with the methodology. The limitations were significant and did change some of the data collection, thereby changing format, focus, and participant pool and selection. However, even with limitations placed on the initial study, relevant data was collected, analyzed, and found to be significant in the research.

Specific to the focus groups, limitations were space, the time slot provided to the researcher, and communication to the participants of the larger summit with regard to the research and opportunity to participate in the focus group. Change of location or limited space impaired interested parties' attempts to participate. The initial proposal stated Teach to Lead would share communications with participants from the researcher as approved by the committee, or members within, but would not provide a list of participants or e-mails; and Teach to Lead would work to embed the research in the regular summit (room, equipment, time, collection of data) without deterring or impeding on the agenda or focus of the summit.

A major limitation of the survey was that initially the link was to be provided to all summit participants. With the organizing committee changing for each summit, there was a lack of communication where both the survey and focus groups were left out of initial plans. In addition, there was a change of administration as an election year, which also created a hiccup in communication and follow-through of the initial proposal. Rather than have all participants of every summit included, which was an estimated 130 people per summit and five summits attended, the number significantly reduced to include only those who took the time after the summit to complete the survey.

In the initial proposal, the interviews were to be held with summit attendees who authorized follow-up when they participated in a thirty-sixty-ninety day interview through Teach to Lead. A limitation to the interviews was even though all three organizations had representation and discussion with the researcher specific to the interview, it was later decided not to provide the researcher with any contact information. Therefore, the initial interview plan was then changed, both in format and content. In format, only those identified or who volunteered to participate were included; and in content in that the questions were specific to teacher leader impact on students, colleagues, and district or school.

A connected limitation is teachers' failure to step up to use their voice when provided the opportunity. Invitations to participate in the research (both the survey and the interviews) were sent to all contacts made at the Teach to Lead summit. Invitations were also sent to all students—past and present—connected with the master's or doctoral degrees in teacher leadership at a specific university. In addition, invitations were sent out to students taking courses specific to teacher leadership by the program leader of the teacher leadership program at the same institution. Social media was also used to encourage participation, providing the link to the survey and promise of anonymity if desired. However, participation proved low.

ANALYSIS, SYNTHESIS, AND EVALUATION OF THE DATA

Data analysis occurred in stages and were specific to the methodology. In each area, the analysis assisted with the understanding of the participants' experiences, and consequent trends and patterns within the field.

The survey was completed electronically through a commercial site. Data was collected for one year and an analysis was provided through the company. Interpretation and reporting of this analysis is shared in this chapter. Focus groups were held only face-to-face, and only at one time as determined within the schedule of the Teach to Lead summit at which it was collected. Notes were taken by the researcher, which were later coded and categorized. Specific to the interviews, the researcher carefully listened to each interview multiple times and then had them transcribed. Open coding was followed by collaborative discussion between researchers specific to the data collected.

The researchers began to notice things and think things (Seidel 1998). Analysis of the data brought the researchers to the following conclusions:

- The exploration of teacher leadership through the lens of district and schools has shown a great variance in both definition and role. Only one district of all those surveyed or interviewed had a formal definition of teacher leadership. This shows that educators need to be introspective to both limitations and possibilities of teacher leadership and explore essential components of teacher leadership that might open or advance possibilities.

- Teacher leaders were encouraged to share their voice through multiple methodologies. An observation made is as the questions moved to *impact*, *policy*, or *voice*, there were fewer responses provided. This corroborates the fact that there are areas where teacher leaders feel ill-equipped, or hesitant to speak out or act.
- Examination of the culture created for teacher leadership highlights the importance of the building administrator. Creating a positive culture that embraces teacher leadership, focuses on effective and frequent communication, communicating and upholding core values, shared vision, developing the foundation for change and success, honoring tradition, recognizing and celebrating everyday heroes and heroines, and keeping the focus on the students.
- Culture incorporates the complexity of relationships between principal and teacher leader, teacher leader to teacher leader, and teacher leader to teacher. Professional relationships can be enhanced or impeded through fostering a culture that encourages risk taking. One must not be penalized for taking risks and thinking outside the box if that's what is needed and expected.
- Culture also includes the illumination of recognition of the significance of contributions to the classroom and the school. Recognition can be accomplished at staff meetings, but is encouraged to extend beyond to include evaluations, board meetings, annual reports for school improvement and such. Therefore, creative extension beyond recognition by name calls for substantiated collaboration giving credit to the group as well as the individual leading.

Investigation of the roles and responsibilities of teacher leaders has shown that these are dependent on the district/school. While many districts and schools utilize teacher leaders in same or similar capacities, there are no defined job descriptions, much less a common definition of teacher leader.

Regarding preparation, the findings are that most districts do not have a requirement for formal education nor endorsement for teacher leadership. In addition, most districts do not have nor require specific professional development for the teacher leader to assume or step into additional duties. Therefore, it becomes necessary for each district and school to define teacher leaders in such a way that represents them, and their needs. While often this comes down to roles and responsibilities, the measure should come down to skills and processes.

In addition, while the teacher leaders are performing in these roles, they must not only build capacity in their colleagues and students, but in themselves. Thus, a reliable measure of effectiveness must be established, and with this is evidence of impact on student learning, colleagues, and districts and schools. As the researchers synthesized the findings as they relate to current practices in teacher leadership, the following considerations were made:

- An area of significance that was highlighted is *resources*, which includes but extends beyond financial support.
- To further development of teacher leaders, in addition to *focus on student learning* is *teacher leaders' impact on colleagues*. This calls for teacher leaders to advocate for the growth and development of teachers as well as students, and build capacity in others.
- The design of *The Framework for Effective Teacher Leadership* offers specific indicators to increase introspection for selection, preparation, and retention of teacher leaders. In a larger context, it provides awareness and accountability to increase teacher learning and growth, teacher satisfaction, student learning, and school improvement.
- Further thinking needs to take place on how to champion, advocate for, and retain teacher leaders who shoulder responsibilities for the greater good, as well as how this could be done more efficiently and effectively.
- Recommended change includes creating, communicating, and encouraging career pathways reflecting a lattice approach where movement can take place fluidly, presenting opportunity for teachers rather than a stagnant field.
- Further exploration and development of culture that embraces teacher leader impact, voice, and policy changes.
- Development, implementation, and monitoring of recruitment of a diverse group of teacher leaders.
- Encourage open discussion between administrative organizations and higher education to address the apprehension of administration to empower teacher leaders or follow shared or distributed leadership with fidelity due to accountability. To improve, we need definitive boundaries with tough conversations taking place prior to teachers moving into teacher leader positions. Rather than micromanage situations, administrators must let go of what is comfortable, and embrace the possibilities of what could be. However, it is recognized that district-level administration, boards, and communities must have an understanding of what the principal is, and is not, accountable for if shared or distributed leadership is implemented and supported. Furthermore, principal-preparation programs must educate upcoming administrators on how to work with, communicate with, empower, and effectively utilize teacher leaders.

Teacher leaders are change agents, and promote reason and impetus for advancement of initiatives, ideas, interests, skills, and talents. Teacher leaders identify and analyze a change in practice that causes a reexamination of belief or change of a mindset beyond an adjustment of time or change of a mindset.

Teacher leaders create and explore opportunities through delving deeper into tough conversations with colleagues, such as meeting our students where they are or providing students with necessary resources versus a mindset of attributing lack of performance to race, gender, or socioeconomic identifiers. With this comes an understanding that conflict is not bad, and may be the spark or impetus for change.

Emphasized in teacher leadership is the formulation of common language and intentional practice of shared or distributed leadership that supports collective wisdom and celebrates the knowledge, skills, dispositions, and practices of each member. To defend the position to build capacity in self and others, the culture must be one that encourages risk-taking and supports the person's vision and efforts over results.

RECOMMENDATIONS FOR THE FUTURE

The survey suggests the number of participants consistently declined answering questions as they became more specific to impact, policy, and voice. Following are some considerations for further thought and research:

- Does the perception match the reality specific to perceived impact of teacher leaders on student achievement, colleagues, and school/district?
- What is the level of understanding teachers have of current school policy, specific to their own placement?
- Do teachers have, and use, their voices to advocate, change, and/or generate school policy?
- What is the confidence level of teachers to advocate for, change, and/ or generate school policy?

Recommendations for further research stemming from the focus groups include:

- What evidence is available specific to how monies/resources have been utilized (including Title II/Every Student Succeeds Act funding)?
- Is the professional development/training offered effective?
- What evidence do we have that professional development has made a difference in student achievement or impacted instruction?

Recommendations for further research stemming from the interviews and discussions include:

- Are teacher leaders effectively prepared for success in the roles and responsibilities assigned, appointed, or assumed?
- How can we share the profession through the light that teacher leadership is a career pathway, and teaching is not a flat profession (thus increasing recruitment and retention numbers in the field)?
- What needs to take place, whether at the national, state, or local levels and with higher education institutions involved, to diversify the teacher leader workforce?
- How can we better educate students, meeting them where they are and understanding the trauma some endure before they even reach the doors of the school?

Throughout the discussions and interviews held, one question repeatedly surfaced: are all great teachers then great leaders? Teachers may be highly effective in the classroom, but teacher leadership calls for a definitive set of leadership skills different than those of a classroom teacher.

Teacher leaders are often viewed as the bridge or liaisons between teachers and administrators; therefore, they must have and use skills from both skill sets. Since teacher leadership is a skill set, if we train teachers, then expose them to these opportunities and allow them to practice these skills, then all teachers can potentially grow into leaders. This approach calls for a systemic change that offers a safe, nonjudgmental, and risk-taking environment. It calls for the district or school to strengthen and build up the skills of adults, and for administration to both recognize and utilize teacher leaders.

Steven Miller, principal at Graham Elementary, Springfield 186 (IL) captured this when he stated in his interview, "all teachers have the ability to lead somewhere. I just have to find it. I have to find what their passion is, what they're good at . . . It's about getting to know my staff so that I work to their strengths because everyone has a strength—I just have to find it and build on it" (personal communication, October 25, 2017).

SUMMARY

This chapter focuses on research conducted with practitioners in the field. Through data and evidence, there is confirmation of past studies and a revelation of current practices. Consistent with literature dating back to the 1980s, teacher leadership has no common definition nor placement on a salary scale specific to position, roles and responsibilities vary, the selection process is left to the local system, and teacher leaders are most often evaluated as classroom teachers without accountability, stipend, or recognition of additional service.

To date, most districts and schools do not require a formal education or state certification to undertake these roles and responsibilities. However, interviews and discussion reveal that those who have participated in a formal program self-identify as having grown exponentially. Formally prepared teachers have a far greater understanding of the role of the administrator and reasons for changes or initiatives, and are better at the skills required for the roles and responsibilities they have undertaken as a teacher leader; for example, data analysis, school-wide assessment, developing professional development meaningful to all, and so on, thereby making it easier to support their administration, have positive conversations with colleagues, understand what is taking place building-wide, and supporting school-wide goals.

Mark Doan, superintendent of Effingham Unit 40, stated, "Just do one thing: let your staff know they *can* try new things . . . I'll never have the finances for instructional coaches or other specific roles, but I can build capacity in my teachers" (personal communication, January 23, 2018).

Also stemming from discussions and interviews is the fact that teacher leadership is ripe, meaning it has resurfaced with interest and possibilities of financial support through such funds as Title II/ESSA. It is now up to educators themselves to shift the paradigm. We have all heard the cliché attributed to Albert Einstein, that the definition of insanity is doing the same thing over and over and expecting a different result. It's now our time—make it different.

SELF-ASSESSMENT AND REFLECTION

Reflect on your school. Consider your current position. Contemplate where you are, and where you see yourself in three, five, and ten years. If you are currently a teacher or teacher leader, have you considered what skills you can share with colleagues? What are your interests? Your passions? What is your current impact on student learning? How do you contribute to the school or district? How do you contribute to state policies and procedures?

Revisit *The Framework for Effective Teacher Leadership*, and reflectively discern possibilities. If you are currently an administrator, school or district leader, or other supporter such as a board or community member, reflect on ways you can support, or better support, the teachers and teacher leaders in the district you serve. Be intentional and specific to help grow internal leaders, encourage them, support them, and celebrate their accomplishments.

REFERENCES

Dalton, J. and Smith, D. (1986). *Extending children's special abilities: Strategies for primary classrooms*. Melbourne, Australia: Curriculum Branch, Schools Division.

Danielson, C. (2011). *The framework for teaching evaluation instrument*. Princeton, NJ: The Danielson Group LLC.

Denzin, N. K. (1989). *Interpretive interactionism*. Newbury Park, CA: Sage Publications.

Seidel, J. V. (1998). *Qualitative data analysis in the ethnograph*, v5.0. Colorado Springs, CO: Qualis Research.

Strike, K., Sims, P., Mann, S., and Wilhite, R. (2016). *Transforming professional practice: A framework for effective leadership*. Lanham, MD: Rowman & Littlefield.

UNESCO. (2008). Understanding and Using the ILO/UNESCO Recommendation concerning the Status of Teachers (1966) and the UNESCO Recommendation concerning the Status of Higher-Education Teaching Personnel (1997). Paris, France: United Nations Educational, Scientific and Cultural Organization and International Labour Organization (UNESCO).

York-Barr, J. and Duke, K. (2004, Fall). What do we know about teacher leadership? Findings from two decades of scholarship. *Review of Educational Research 74*(3): 255–316.

ACKNOWLEDGMENTS

The researchers wish to acknowledge and celebrate the people who took the time to share their voice. It is with much appreciation and great respect that the following are recognized for their contributions to the research conducted for *The Framework for Effective Teacher Leadership*:

Chelle Beck–Curriculum Director, Effingham Unit 40	Illinois
Steven Miller–Principal, Springfield 186	Illinois
Kelli Koch–Instructional Coach, Pickerington Local School District	Ohio
Michelle Stone–Instructional Coach, Pickerington Local School District	Ohio
Terry Logan-Mottinger–Art Specialist, Columbus City Schools	Ohio
Amber Gresham–Third Grade Teacher, Columbus City Schools	Ohio
Blythe Wood–Academic/Behavior Coach (SPED), Pickerington Local School District	Ohio
Joe Fatheree–High School Teacher, Effingham Unit 40	Illinois

Pablo Pitcher DeProto–Teacher, Oakland Unified School District — California
Lisa Carey–Instructional Support Teacher, Hoover City Schools — Alabama
Renee Scott–Education Program Consultant, SEA — Kentucky
Stacey Gibson–Consultant, Chicago — Illinois
Kelsey Lewis–First Grade Teacher, Lee County School District — Florida
Teresa Lien–District Instructional Facilitator, Baraboo School District — Wisconsin
Jane McMahon–K12 Instructional Coach, Baraboo School District — Wisconsin
Rebecca Binion–Fifth Grade Teacher, Oklahoma Public Schools — Oklahoma
Lori Spinelli-Samara–Educational Consultant — Washington, DC
Charlotte Wellen–Teacher, Albemarle County Public Schools — Virginia
DeHannah Ehrli–Special Education, Orange County Public Schools — Florida
Stephanie Thomas–Instructional Support, Orange County Public Schools — Florida
Judy Levin–Faculty, University of Central Florida — Florida
Joanna Barney–Third Grade Teacher, North Thurston School District — Washington
Erin Whitlock–Consultant, Professional Practice — Oregon
Ashley Landes- Spanish Teacher, Hillsborough County Public Schools — Florida
Ingrid Cumming–Instructional Support (ESE), Orange County Public Schools — Florida
Pamela Bradley–HS Teacher, Simi Valley — California
Sama Hashime–Art Teacher, Fairfax County Public Schools — Virginia
Libya Doman–Art Teacher, Fairfax County Public Schools — Virginia

Others wished not to have their names published or participated anonymously in the survey.

In addition to these individuals, it is with sincere gratitude to the following for their support specific to time, space, expertise, and further connections as we plan for the future of teacher leadership:

Teach to Lead
US Department of Education–Ruthanne Buck, Maddie Fennell and Vanessa Tesoriero
Association of Supervision and Curriculum Development (ASCD)
National Board for Professional Teaching Standards (NBPTS)–Tami Fitzgerald
Roger Eddy–Illinois State Representative District 109
Katherine Bassett–President/CEO, National Network of State Teachers of the Year (NNSTOY)
Audrey Soglin–Executive Director, Illinois Education Association (IEA)
Mark Doan–Superintendent, Effingham Unit 40, Illinois

Appendix A

Survey Questions

QUESTIONS FOR OPEN-ENDED RESPONSE SURVEY

Italics identify connection to The Framework for Effective Teacher Leadership:

Domain I—Teacher Leader Competencies

- Explain how teacher leaders model accountability and responsibility in your district/school.
- Explain how teacher leaders have created and supported change.

Domain II—Relational Leadership

- Provide specific example(s) of characteristics of the teacher leader as Master teacher, and how this impacts relationships with colleagues.
- Describe the impact teacher leaders have on the collaboration of teachers and administrators, and the effects on the culture and climate of your school.

Domain III—Instructional Leadership

- Provide specific examples of guidance provided by teacher leaders with regard to coaching, mentoring, and modeling and how it impacts student learning.
- Describe how teacher leaders use assessments and data to drive decision making.

Domain IV—Management Skills

- Provide specific examples of how teacher leaders harness the skills, expertise, and knowledge of colleagues in your building.
- Describe how teacher leaders in your building understand, respond to, and influence the larger political, social, economic, legal, and cultural context.

General

- In an "elevator conversation" how would you summarize the benefits of teacher leaders to a stakeholder?
- What limitations are placed on teacher leaders, and by whom?

QUESTIONS FOR CLOSED RESPONSE

General Questions

Name of School
City and State of School

Which best describes roles **assumed** by teacher leaders in your district? (check all that apply)

- Mentor
- Instructional coach
- Data coach
- Professional development organizer
- Teacher evaluator
- Director
- Team lead/grade lead
- Dean
- Chair
- Researcher
- Policy maker
- Voice in decision making
- Union representative
- Other (please list below)

Which best describes roles **assigned or appointed** to teacher leaders in your district? (check all that apply)

- Mentor
- Instructional coach
- Data coach
- Professional development organizer
- Teacher evaluator
- Director
- Team lead/grade lead
- Dean
- Chair
- Researcher
- Policy maker
- Voice in decision making
- Union representative
- Other (please list below)

Please select methods of support you find most useful (check all that apply):

- Phone/e-mail contact
- Individual check-in
- Webinars
- Labs/physical follow-up
- Data access
- FAQ document
- Professional Learning Communities
- Online sources on my own (i.e., Teachers Pay Teachers)
- Other (please identify below)

For the purpose of this survey, *Teacher Leadership* is defined as, "Transformative action yielding significant and sustainable results through support by teachers to teachers to improve the effectiveness of teaching and learning, and promote and influence change to improve school and student outcomes" (Strike 2016).

Likert Scale: *Strongly Disagree; Disagree; Neither Disagree or Agree; Agree; Strongly Agree; NA Does Not Apply*

Structural Factors

The role of teacher leaders in your school is formal and reflected in areas such as title, selection, official capacity, authority, and payment.

The role of teacher leaders in your school is informal in that they emerge, influence with persuasion and without authority, have a voice without final say, and do so without compensation.

Responsibilities of teacher leaders are clearly stated through a written job description.

There is a clearly defined evaluation system specific to teacher leaders in my district.

There are clearly defined knowledge, skills, dispositions, and practices specific to teacher leaders that are clearly defined and supported by the district.

Teacher leaders listen to the colleagues they represent.

Teacher leaders have the ear of administrators.

Teach leaders have an active voice in decision making.

Teacher leaders are allocated time, professional learning opportunities, finances, material, and personnel.

Teacher leaders are provided opportunities through the district to learn necessary skills for exercising leadership.

Teacher leaders have received comprehensive training/professional development on the use of data to drive instruction.

Cultural Factors

Teacher leaders are encouraged to visit classrooms, and are provided the time to do so.

Teacher leaders are valued as professionals.

Teacher leaders work collaboratively with school administrators.

Teacher leaders are provided time for collaboration within the normal contract day.

Teacher leaders advocate for student needs.

Teacher leaders are actively encouraged to take risks and propose new ideas.

Teacher leaders are called upon for their input, expertise, training, or instructional leadership.

The district/school shares opportunities, acknowledges, celebrates, and rewards teacher leaders.

Likert Scale: *Strongly Disagree; Disagree; Neither Disagree or Agree; Agree; Strongly Agree; NA, Does Not Apply; DK, I don't know*

Perceptions

The **US Department of Education** recognizes the importance of teacher leaders and provides support through education and/or training.

The **US Department of Education** recognizes the importance of teacher leaders and provides support through allocation of funds.

The **State Department of Education** recognizes the importance of teacher leaders and provides support through education and/or training.

The **State Department of Education** recognizes the importance of teacher leaders and provides support through allocation of funds.

District leadership recognizes the importance of teacher leaders and provides support through education and/or training.

District leadership recognizes the importance of teacher leaders and provides support through allocation of funds.

Building leadership recognizes the importance of teacher leaders and provides support through education and/or training.

Building leadership recognizes the importance of teacher leaders and provides support through allocation of funds.

The **Local Board of Education** recognizes the importance of teacher leaders and provides support through education and/or training.

The **Local Board of Education** recognizes the importance of teacher leaders and provides support through allocation of funds.

The Union recognizes the importance of teacher leaders and provides support through education and/or training.

The Union recognizes the importance of teacher leaders and provides support through allocation of funds.

Other teachers in my building, grade level, or department recognize the importance of teacher leaders and provide support.

Higher Education Institutions recognize the importance of teacher leaders and provides support.

Area nonprofit organizations recognize the importance of teacher leaders and provide support.

Selection

There is a known selection process to undertake a role in teacher leadership in your school.

There are known criteria to undertake a role in teacher leadership in your school.

Teachers have a voice in selection of those moving into a teacher leadership role.

Those serving in teacher leader roles are reflective practitioners.
Those serving in teacher leader roles are open to input and feedback.
Those serving in teacher leader roles are collaborative in nature.
Those serving in teacher leader roles are transparent.
Those serving in teacher leader roles are ethical.
Those serving in teacher leader roles work well with both administrators and teachers.
Those serving in teacher leader roles understand and effectively use data.
Those serving in teacher leader roles demonstrate self-knowledge as critical to their development and success.
Those serving in teacher leader roles are involved in a comprehensive professional growth plan.
Those serving in teacher leader roles are required to complete a license/endorsement program from an accredited program.
Those serving in teacher leader roles have participated in training/professional learning above and beyond the classroom teacher.

Trends

A teacher leader endorsement/license is recognized at state level.
There is a recognized group of standards for teacher leaders in my state.
Communication specific to teacher leadership is provided by our state to our district/school.
The structure and allocated resources within our district supports teacher leaders.
There are specific guidelines provided by the district for teacher leaders.
Policies and procedures related to teacher leadership are clearly stated in my district.
Teacher leaders are active participants in needs assessment, planning, and actions taken by the district.
Teacher leaders are active participants in collection, analysis, and reporting of data.
Student achievement is directly connected to teacher performance in my district.

Rank

Please rank the following sources of influence on teacher leaders in your district:

- Professional development/training
- Curriculum
- Personal reading
- Students
- Colleagues
- Personal experience
- Family
- Leader
- Other (please identify below)

Appendix B

Interview Questions

1. Share with me the **definition** of "teacher leadership" used in your district/school.
2. How are teacher leaders **selected** in your district/school?
   a. Appointed, selected, colleagues move them into position, self-assumed
   b. Is there an identified level of education, formal education (i.e. a program), or state endorsement/certification required?
   c. Does the person need to be approved by leadership, board, or other governing body?
   d. Is there a clearly defined **job description** provided to candidates/new teacher leaders? How does this job description support the district?
   e. What **dispositions** are highlighted by your district/school for teacher leaders?
   f. Describe the logistics of the position in your district/school i.e., classroom teacher with some outside duties; Teacher on Special Assignment (TOSA); hired as teacher leader under different title (Coach, Interventionist, Resource Teacher); has teachers assigned to them to work with; teachers have the option to ask to work with; time is provided and the teacher leader establishes his/her own duties and schedule.
   g. Describe the **relationship** between teacher leaders and administrators.
   h. Describe the **support** provided to teacher leaders, and how that impacts their work.
3. Describe the **communication** skills of teacher leaders, and how they work with others (teachers, admin) to work through resilience, influence timely interventions, support reflective practice, emulate transparency, and/or promote change.

4. Describe the **impact** of teacher leaders specific to **student achievement** (i.e., establish a growth mindset).
5. Describe the **impact** of teacher leaders specific to their **colleagues** (i.e., provide differentiated strategies).
6. Describe the **impact** of teacher leaders specific to their **district/school** (i.e., school culture, creating a positive and/or effective learning environment).
7. Would you say that the **impact** of teacher leaders in these areas (student achievement, colleagues, and district/school) are **sustainable changes**? Why or why not?
8. Share an example of how teacher leaders continuously strive to **improve impact** of teachers on students.
9. Are teacher leaders held **accountable** in your district/school? Specifically describe how they are held accountable, what they are held accountable for, measures of accountability, and what takes place if they are not accountable.
10. Describe the teacher leaders' **role** and involvement specific to the use of data in your district/school, including how it is used to track student performance, intervention plan, monitoring, and use of data to inform instructional practices.
11. How would you describe teacher leaders' effective **collaboration** specific to positive influence on student learning and the learning environment? What **attributes** describe how the group worked together? How do teacher leaders effectively balance autonomy with collective commitment?
12. Describe if and how teacher leaders **impact** the following: challenge the status quo, stretch the thinking of others, advocate, inspire, build resiliency, establish a growth mindset, challenge the thinking of colleagues and leadership, obtain teacher voice, and share decision making.
13. What **contributions** have teacher leaders made in your district, school, and community?
14. What **inspires or encourages** the teacher leaders in your district/school?
15. What **hinders or challenges** teacher leaders in your district/school, or deters others from wanting to take on this role?
16. Share specific training/PD you would like to see for teacher leaders in your district/school (i.e., integrating technology, apps that support instruction, data, instructional strategies, etc.).
17. Is there anything I have not asked that you would like to share with me about teacher leadership?

Index

About the Authors

Kimberly T. Strike, PhD, is professor of education and coordinator of doctoral studies at Southern Wesleyan University, Central, South Carolina. She earned her doctorate at Marquette University in the areas of curriculum, instruction, administration, and supervision with an emphasis on educational technology. She has provided services to public, parochial, choice, and charter schools. She has served as a teacher, teacher leader, principal, director of curriculum and instruction, supervisor of title funds, ELA coordinator in the Regional Office of Education, and professor. Kimberly presented at Carnegie Foundation's Summit for Improvement in Education (2018). In addition to *Identifying and Growing Internal Leaders: A Framework for Effective Teacher Leadership*, she has six other publications through Rowman and Littlefield, including *Transforming Professional Practice: A Framework for Effective Leadership* (2016). Kimberly has served as an educational ambassador to China and earned PDK's Distinguished Leader in Education Award. She continues to work with various educational and service programs through local, national, and international channels. She works with consortiums, committees, and task forces at the local and state levels to advance practice and policy for high-quality programs and to further understanding and effective use of teacher leaders, and has served as a critical friend for Teach to Lead and Powered by Teach to Lead since 2016.

Janis Fitzsimmons, PhD, has taught at North Central College (NCC) since 1985 where she received the college's Dissinger Award for excellence in program development and administration and performance of a job above and beyond the call of duty. In addition to her teaching duties, she is the founder and executive director of the NCC Junior/Senior Scholars Program, the Promise Teacher Corps, and the Urban Education Laboratory, which she currently directs. The Junior/Senior Scholars Program has twice been named an Exemplary Practice by the Illinois Board of Higher Education. In addition, Jan founded and continues to direct the *Center for Success in High-Need Schools*, a collaboration of twenty-three independent colleges and universities who come together monthly to advance recruiting, preparing, and retaining teachers and leaders for at-risk schools. She has worked collaboratively with this group to garner more than seventeen million dollars in grant funds, and has presented at the state and national levels on preparing teachers to succeed in high need schools and assuring opportunity and access for the historically underrepresented students. Jan serves on and leads state task force groups to advance practice and policy for high-quality programs for all, publishes a biannual online journal, and leads an online professional development network for teachers and leaders. Jan has been a special education teacher, curriculum coordinator, and principal. Jan earned her PhD at the University of Chicago in education curriculum and instruction.

Rebecca Hornberger, PhD, is assistant professor in the Department of Leadership at Concordia University Chicago, River Forest, Illinois. She also serves as the department chair of SAIL for Education. SAIL is a partnership between the Ohio Association of Elementary School Administrators (OAESA) and Concordia University Chicago to provide graduate-level coursework that focuses on effective instructional leadership practices for aspiring teacher leaders and building- and district-level leaders throughout Ohio. She earned her doctorate from Concordia University Chicago in the area of educational leadership. She has served as a public school principal and teacher leader for twenty years. She also collaborates with educational leaders throughout the state of Ohio by coordinating professional development and networking and outreach for OAESA. Rebecca worked with stakeholders across Ohio to develop the Ohio Teacher Leadership Framework and to revise the Ohio Teacher Leader Endorsement Standards. She regularly authors a column in OAESA's *Principal Navigator* magazine and works collaboratively with educators throughout the state to advocate for high-quality leadership programs, policies, and support systems.